Environment
Why Read the Classics?

ENVIRONMENT
Why Read the Classics?

Edited by Sofia Guedes Vaz

Routledge
Taylor & Francis Group

LONDON AND NEW YORK

First published 2013 by Greenleaf Publishing Limited

Published 2017 by Routledge
2 Park Square, Milton Park, Abingdon, Oxon OX14 4RN
711 Third Avenue, New York, NY 10017, USA

Routledge is an imprint of the Taylor & Francis Group, an informa business

British Library Cataloguing in Publication Data:
   A catalogue record for this book is available from the British Library.

   ISBN-13: 978-1-906093-75-4 (pbk)

Contents

Foreword

You hold in your hands a series of essays on six classics of environmental literature. These are the building blocks of a movement that has grown in strength and intensity to the point where it challenges received wisdom and offers a path to a different and more sustainable future. They are classics because each of them fulfils four key criteria of classical literature: they have artistic quality, they have stood the test of time, they have universal appeal, and they encourage us to make connections both with each other and with the world around us. But because they are also books that aim to get us to see the world in a different way, they have to fulfil a fifth criterion: they must be persuasive and inspirational. On all five of these counts, the books discussed here definitely merit the status of 'classics', and the essays written about them here match their quality, relevance and timeliness. We can pair these books up and see that each pair has played a crucial role in creating the conditions for thinking differently about the environment and our relationship with it.

Walden and *The Sand County Almanac* introduce a new player to the political and social stage: non-human nature. And the part played by nature on this stage is not a bit part, or merely a backdrop to the main drama—it is a principal character and an actor in its own right. Thoreau and Leopold write philosophy, but not of the traditional sort. We do not find here a series of claims and counterclaims, analyses and syntheses, but a lyrical philosophy which seeks to persuade through the power of observation, story-telling and a heartfelt account of what it is like to live with nature rather than against it.

Silent Spring and *Small is Beautiful* both make us question, in different ways, the nature of progress. Rachel Carson took a brave stand against the use of chemical pesticides in agriculture, forc-ing us to consider the whole impact of our technologies rather than confining our assessment of their success to one sector or aspect of our lives. Progress is not only a matter of *techne* but of ethics, too, and, once Thoreau and Leopold had introduced nature to our ethical debate, the stage was set for the idea of a 'silent spring' to move from being just an alliterative phrase to a powerful description of a diminished and impoverished world.

Schumacher bucks the trend of 'bigger is always better', whether it be cities, companies, or the size of a national economy. What do we want out of life? he asks. And if the answer to this is 'to flour-ish', then we need to ask ourselves questions about the scale of our activity. Schumacher introduces the language of 'appropriate-ness' to our relationship with the world around us and thus pro-vides a key entry into the world of *Limits to Growth*. Published just four years after the iconic photograph taken by the astronauts of *Apollo 8* which showed a blue-and-green Earth hanging in the blackness of space, *Limits* demonstrates the folly of the aspiration to grow our economies without regard for the finite size of the planet on which we live.

Our Common Future adds a further dimension to the planetary and nature-related sensibilities at the core of its five companions: the future. So much of our lives is lived in the present, and so much of our politics and economics is based on short-term cal-culation. Imagine how different things would be if we thought future people counted as much as present people; imagine how 'common sense' would be transformed if the welfare of future generations was as important as our welfare.

And this is what the six classics discussed here do to us: they unsettle common sense, they offer a new perspective of our place in space, in time. They are, in this regard, revolutionary, and we need a revolution of thought and practice if we are to reach the next century, let alone a third millennium, at peace with the natural world.

Andrew Dobson
Keele University, UK

Introduction

Sofia Guedes Vaz

This is a book about books: books that have been an important part of the environmental movement; books that are perhaps classics, green classics—you will decide. In any case, they are special if we consider what Sir Francis Bacon had to say about how to read: 'Read not to contradict and confute, not to believe and take for granted, not to find talk and discourse, but to weigh and consider.' This advice is clearly more appropriate for some books than for others, and the six books examined in the chapters that follow are perfect examples of what Bacon was talking about and the type of book that tends to instigate reflection, above all. These are also books that absorb us and take us to a green world of the imagination which, if we allow it, will seduce and conquer us, not only because they are compelling and beautiful texts, but because they are written in a way that makes us easily identify with their narratives.

Walden, or Life in the Woods, the first book revisited, written by Henry David Thoreau in 1854, takes us on a personal journey of discovery which reminds us that humankind is neither superior nor inferior to nature but rather, above all, an integral part of it. *A Sand County Almanac* follows. This beautiful collection of essays by Aldo Leopold seeks to provide us with reason and motive to care for nature, both in its own right and as an essential element of humanness. In 1962, Rachel Carson's *Silent Spring* was published, becoming and remaining a bestseller throughout the last half of the 20th century. The silence that Carson evokes in this book is actually quite loud; it is a silence that makes us reflect, yet again, on our relationship with nature, but for the worst reason—the absence of birdsong. *The Limits to Growth*, by Meadows, Meadows, Randers and Behrens III, examines the much-reviled and unpopular question of limits. In fact, this book, written in 1972, marked a time when the idea of the unlimited ceased to be (for some of us) a universal form of existence in the world. The fifth book, published one year later, is *Small is Beautiful: Economics as if People Mattered,* written by E.F. Schumacher; it questions the economic structure that dominates the world and makes it so unjust, unsustainable and inefficient. The last book, *Our Common Future*, published in 1987 by the United Nations, pioneered the concept of sustainable development, which endures as one of the most iconic ideas of the environmental movement.

These books are often considered as some of the environmental movement's most emblematic, and quite possibly its primary, promoters. More than just books about the environment, they are also philosophical treatises, in that they increase our understanding of the natural world and of ourselves, calling us 'to weigh and consider', as Bacon put it. In particular, they make us reflect on the need to constantly redefine the purposes of progress, the economy and society. How we relate to nature is a crucial aspect in the plans we make as a species, and as individuals; and every one of these books inspires a more respectful relationship, both with nature and humanity, and consequently with ourselves.

This book is made up of six essays written about the six books. The essays are the result of a series of conferences organised in

Lisbon by the Calouste Gulbenkian Foundation with the support of the American Embassy in Portugal. Its *raison d'être* was the need to revisit the ideas that have shaped the environmental movement, seeking inspiration to deal with what looks like a very challenging future. The significance of such timeless concepts is now more apparent than ever; and these evergreen books are full of ideas that retain their spark even in our difficult times. This is what makes them classics.

Green classics

The initial list for this project included many more texts, books and authors that could be considered 'pioneering' within the environmental movement. In fact, the six books could have been 60. However, after much discussion, these six were finally selected because, individually and collectively, they tell the most important 'green' narratives regarding what we need to know about relationships between nature, environment and ourselves. It is the range of emotions and intellectual engagement they offer that has led us to designate them as classics. And the title of this book was inspired by Italo Calvino's *Why Read the Classics?*,[1] in which he offers 14 different definitions of what might be considered a classic text.

The six books analysed in this volume fit some of these definitions; and we could start with one definition that is both comprehensive and something that maps out the universe of what we wanted to share with the public of our conferences and with you, the reader. 'The classics are books which exercise a particular influence, both when they imprint themselves on our imagination as unforgettable, and when they hide in the layers of memory disguised as the individual's or the collective unconscious';[2] this is the reason why many of these books are often cited as those that have influenced, and still influence, the environmental movement. *Silent Spring* is often considered to be the book that started the environmental movement in the first place. However, all of the narratives, which are either romantic (the first four) or more pragmatic (the last two) in scope, are imprinted on the collective 'green' imagination of Western societies. Even for those who have never read them, constant citations and references make them seem familiar and, in a way, a sort of heritage of what one identifies with a green consciousness.

However, even if they sound familiar, and their arguments sometimes a little tired, do not think that if you read them you will not be surprised, because, as another of Calvino's definitions points out, 'Classics are books which, the more we think we know them through hearsay, the more original, unexpected, and innovative we find them when we actually read them.'[3] So do not be put off if you know off by heart the most-cited definition of sustainable development given in *Our Common Future*. The report's structure, concepts and philosophy may still impress you if you approach it with an open mind. Reading *Walden* for the first time makes you curious about who Thoreau was, and how genuine he might be. You might re-read it and always find something new in Thoreau's ability to be both a real philosopher, in the sense that he thought deeply about ethical issues, and at the same time a simple man living with nature. It may be a new experience to feel the author's life and his narrative as a single project. Thoreau observes the real world and the book is as much about him as an observer as it is about what he observes, both the natural world and his contemporary society. Rachel Carson, too, starts chapters with a familiar-sounding story that eventually paves the way to a denouncement of serious environmental problems. The problems may be different from those that afflict us today but they reflect the fundamentally flawed relationship we have with nature and, in the end, this may be the root of all environmental problems, both then and now. So, as Calvino says, these and the other books in this collection are indeed innovative and surprise us at the turn of the page with yet another way of looking at nature, a new thought, a timely analysis or remark that make one think they could have been written just yesterday.

The particular features of these books make them a rich source of ideas, strange though it may sound to search for new ideas in books written so many years ago, and in such different circumstances. The environmental movement has been through different phases, each one shaped by the particular dominant context of the time. And for different individuals, the environmental movement has been different, depending on their own concerns and definitions of the environmental crisis. Nevertheless, and as Calvino also says: 'A classic is a work which persists as background noise even when a present that is totally incompatible with it holds sway.'[4] And the background noise of these books is always the same, and may essentially be a more respectful and responsible relationship with nature and humanity. The six books keep on playing this background music, which might never become a hit, but which never goes out of fashion.

These particular books also have the power to make as much sense in the present as they did when they were written, sometimes even more so, considering that they were, generally, ahead of their time. The need to think about and establish limits, as in *The Limits to Growth,* is an idea that is now gaining more attention than it did back in the 1970s. Our current economic, financial and environmental crisis is inspiring concepts, such as steady-state and de-growth, which are based on the acknowledgement and acceptance of limits. This situation and these circumstances continue to make *The Limits to Growth* compelling reading, or as Calvino would say: 'A classic is a work which relegates the noise of the present to a background hum, which at the same time the classics cannot exist without.'

Another definition that resonates with *Walden, or Life in the Woods* and *A Sand County Almanac*, for example, is 'A classic is a book which has never exhausted all it has to say to its readers.'[5] *Walden* is a book that can be read and re-read, and each time it brings something new, a feeling that something else might have been missed. *A Sand County Almanac* is also a rich, timeless and endless work of art, as the dozens of books and hundreds of papers about it from the past 50 years attest. *Small is Beautiful* is also a plentiful source of concepts, such as its subtitle—*Economics as if People Mattered*—which has been reused recently, due to its particular relevance in a world that has lost contact with reality. Schumacher was an economist who thought like a philosopher, and in writing this book he brought that dimension back to life. In our current crisis, we should re-read *Small is Beautiful* to inspire us to look at the economic system from a broader perspective which moves the focus away from a narrow obsession with GDP, as its richness has not yet 'exhausted all it has to say to its readers'.[6]

Italo Calvino's definitions help us contextualise the importance of these books and legitimate their ranking as environmental classics. The following six essays are presented to better understand what these books are all about and why we should keep them on our shelves, and to encourage people to read or revisit them.

The essays and their authors

The series of conferences that inspired this book went on for some months. Each conference was devoted to one of the books, with a speaker and a commentator. Each speaker was invited to write and present an essay on the chosen text and to improve the essay after the comments and discussion generated at the conference. This book is the outcome of that process.

Walden, or Life in the Woods inaugurated the series. Viriato Soromenho-Marques, a Portuguese professor of philosophy and environmental philosophy, wrote the first essay. His philosophical background is evident throughout the essay, and he looks both at Thoreau and *Walden* through this reflexive perspective. He does not hide his enchantment with Thoreau's experience of living in a cabin for two years, illustrating it as a philosophical journey of self-discovery and the development of personal autonomy. Soromenho-Marques captures very well how Thoreau combines moral integrity with intellectual, physical and naturalist abilities and how, together, these give him a privileged position in analysing both worlds and grant him an allure that makes him a man ahead of his times and perhaps even of our own. The essay tells us how Thoreau's detailed knowledge of nature assists him in his reflections about issues of both ethics and nature, in a way that reminds us just how much we are part of nature. In the beautiful expression 'justice is society's surrogate for beauty', Soromenho-Marques apprehends Thoreau's life project, which involves both fighting for justice in the human world and observing and understanding nature's many complexities and beauty. The essay finishes with what Soromenho-Marques sees as the author's main strength in making *Walden* both an academic and a popular book, which has been able to survive unscathed for over 150 years. Thoreau's firm belief in '*life as both an ethical and aesthetical endeavor*' is present in all Walden's pages.

John Baird Callicott, an active ambassador for *A Sand County Almanac* and Leopold's land ethics legacy, wrote and presented an essay (yet another, after the many he has already produced about the author and the subject), demonstrating that a classic can always be revisited and something new always found. In this essay, Callicott guides us through Leopold's journey in writing and publishing *A Sand County Almanac,* pointing out how difficult it was to get it accepted, due to its lack of unity and for being much more than a book of timely and interesting nature observations, as originally requested by the publishers. The book was eventually published, posthumously, and became a classic of conservation philosophy. Callicott believes, as did Leopold at the time, that lack of unity was an unfounded criticism, as the book follows a thread that gives it its spinal cord and is possibly the cause of its success over the last 60 years: 'the exposition and promulgation of an evolutionary-ecological worldview and its axiological (ethical and aesthetical) and normative (practical moral) implications'. Leopold's ambitious project of suggesting a 'worldview remediation' presented a radical change from the existing 'optimism and self-satisfaction' that characterised American society in the 1950s. Callicott reminds us that Leopold, just as Thoreau before him, opposed the general view of the non-respectful relationship of humans with nature, insisting that, as long as we do not see 'land as a community to which we belong' and 'use it with love and respect', we will not attain any type of harmony in our co-existence on this Earth.

Another feature that Callicott focuses on is the power of the language used by Leopold, which makes the book much more poignant and powerful than others in the same style. Even though Leopold opposed the biblical worldview, 'our Abrahamic concept of land', Callicott defends his use of the Bible's rhetorical power to give strength to his own 'beliefs' about the changed paradigm of our locus in the world. Callicott shows how, in several chapters, Leopold 'indulges in the anthropomorphic personification of other animals' as a way to demystify the divide between animals and humans. Following Leopold's evolutionary-ecological worldview, this essay enlightens us on the importance that this book had, in terms of a non-anthropocentric understanding of the world, and how Leopold, though not a philosopher, was able to lay the foundations of much of the environmental philosophy discipline that has been steadily growing for the past 50 years. Leopold never explicitly talks about the intrinsic value of nature, but this can be read between the lines of this classic. In fact, it is

John Baird Callicott who has devoted his philosophical and academic life to expanding and developing land ethics. Callicott has been, in recent decades, philosophically developing the mindset of the naturalist Aldo Leopold and he finishes his essay with a challenge for us to continue this work. 'To articulate a coherent evolutionary-ecological worldview and work through its axiological and normative implications' remains, Callicott believes, with our increasing knowledge of science, a stimulating task ahead. As Calvino said, a classic never stops providing us with new material.

José Manuel Lima Santos, a Portuguese professor of agricultural economy, was responsible for the essay on *Silent Spring*. Lima Santos guides us through the context in which *Silent Spring* appears, where post-world-war euphoria with science and technology, and all the material comfort they gave to Western populations, blinded us to a careful analysis of unintended consequences. The production of food was imperative and the development of both fertilisers and pesticides allowed productivity to increase exponentially. Humankind was finally dominating Nature and partially achieving what Francis Bacon, in his utopian *New Atlantis* of 1624, foresaw: 'the end of our foundation [the house of Solomon] is the knowledge of causes and secret motions of things, and the enlarging of the bounds of human empire, to the effecting of all things possible'. In 1962, when *Silent Spring* was written, this particular project of science was still largely unquestioned, which is why Rachel Carson, who was the first to so publicly denounce it, is considered a pioneer of the environmental movement.

Lima Santos's essay, which is subtitled 'a legacy for sustainable development', illustrates Carson's courage, pertinence, and a sound exposition of the consequences, for both health and the environment, of such a Baconian project of science. Carson's project is nowadays seen as natural; however, Lima Santos reminds us that, back in the 1960s, she was an absolute and almost isolated pioneer in highlighting the drawbacks of the extensive and unlimited use of pesticides, in particular DDT. More than a simple contribution to studying the consequences of chemicals in the environment, *Silent Spring,* above all, is a masterpiece of science communication, shifting the debate from closed circles to civil society. Lima Santos highlights this facet of Rachel Carson, that she is both a scientist and a writer. *Silent Spring* is not a book about biology, environment or chemicals; it is, essentially, a popular science book—a book that communicates science, not only in a way that everybody understands, but also in a literary way that convinces with its fluidity and clarity.

This essay reminds us that it was this characteristic, together with the soundness of its arguments, that made *Silent Spring* the promoter of the environmental movement, with millions of people reading it and voicing their concerns about the indiscriminate use of chemicals in our environment. Its popularity might have been the first stumbling block for science and technology's status as the panacea for everything. Its impact changed and launched environmental policy. However, *Silent Spring* is also a classic, because, as Lima Santos says, 'Carson developed many ideas that are still relevant to the many challenges and dilemmas we face today, when attempting to create a more sustainable future.'

Lima Santos points out that *Silent Spring* marked the environmental agenda by discussing what he feels are, or should be, its main five main elements: the role of science; the need for a humble science; the public's right to know; the role of scientists in communicating science; and the interplay of truth, interest and economic incentives in the development of science. One must also add the role of the powerful, beautiful, poetic and evocative title that Carson chose for her book.

Tim O'Riordan, a retired British emeritus professor of environmental sciences, was responsible for *The Limits to Growth* conference and essay. O'Riordan himself has been a pioneer of environmental sciences, having focused his academic research career on the institutional aspects of global environmental change policy and practice. His re-reading of *The Limits to Growth* highlights it, just as Lima Santos does for *Silent Spring*, as a masterpiece of science communication (having sold 12 million copies in 30 languages). It had a powerful and, for the most, an unpopular message: a message outlining the need for limits. Humans have a schizophrenic stance towards the concept of limits. While we acknowledge the existence of limits, we do not believe in them until we are faced with them.

This book heralds a time when the future starts being as important as the present, bringing substance to the theme of the next generation, a favourite of environmental philosophers and the most powerful argument for questioning the skewed relationship humans have with nature. As O'Riordan points out, this book was the first to use scenarios in environmental policy-making and as an influential tool to analyse where we are and where we want to go. The use of a complex computer-based model to build these scenarios is this book's great achievement but at the same time possibly its Achilles heel. Yet, as the essay tells us, the impressive accuracy of the results calculated in 1972, especially at the level of trends, shows the importance of this type of exercise in creating discussion and reflection about environmental situations which, in general terms, are even worse now than they were then.

O'Riordan downplays the criticism that this book is gloomy, believing it to be an optimistic book because it charts ways of redesigning realities. Basically, it was not a book predicting doom; it was, above all, a book offering choices, claiming that we needed to change the course of events if we did not want to encounter limits. As such, O'Riordan defends this book as initiating 'the era on global environment change and the emergence of sustainability' and it was, therefore, the precursor of many concepts that now constitute the basis of environmental governance.

Like all the books in this collection, it also 'makes the case for wholesale transformation of human values, compassion, equality of opportunity and of flourishing', as O'Riordan puts it.

'The concept of limits troubles society' says O'Riordan and it is the introduction of this concept in environmental discourse that has been this book's main achievement. It has been downplayed, ignored and mocked but it is now coming from several directions. O'Riordan cites the nine planet boundaries recently identified, reviving this book's message of 40 years ago. The reinvigoration of the steady-state movement and the emergence of a philosophical, political and economic de-growth movement also show how the concept of limits is eventually colonising not only our environmental discourse but also our understanding of possible futures. O'Riordan finishes his essay with a very positive thought on where the word 'unlimited' should rule: 'there are no limits to our transcendental transformation'.

The British-Indian Satish Kumar is a charismatic character with a life journey dedicated to harmony with nature. He has been director of the Schumacher College, which is an alternative college based on the ideals of *Small is Beautiful*. A former monk and long-term peace and environment activist, in the 1960s Satish Kumar embarked on an 8,000-mile peace pilgrimage, walking from India to America, via Moscow, London and Paris. Kumar met Schumacher and says in his essay that it was he who convinced him to be the editor of the journal *Resurgence*, a post that he still holds today.

Schumacher inspired Kumar, as he has inspired many of us over the past 40 years, and his essay pays tribute to that stimulus that shaped much of his own life. Schumacher was able to be a practical and an intellectual man at the same time, says Kumar, who himself followed that path. Kumar develops his essay around the concept of scales. The apt title *Small is Beautiful* immediately sets the agenda Schumacher had in mind. The human scale has been lost in the immensity of globalisation, economy and policy, and needs to be recovered in a way that dignifies humankind. Kumar reminds us that smallness is not the same as narrowness and that Schumacher's main point was finding the appropriate scale.

This fifth essay takes us on a journey of finding the different but most appropriate scales for a dynamic but balanced world. Kumar starts with the scale of human settlements. We now have more than half the population of the world living in cities, often enormous cities, which completely destroys the balance between rural and urban. The next encounter is with the economy of scale. Achieving a balance between local and globalised economies was and still is one of the most difficult challenges of economy, or, as Kumar puts it, 'in the name of the economy of scale we ignore the diseconomies of scale'.

The essay then moves on to one of the dimensions dear to both Schumacher and Kumar: the psychology of scale, which is linked with emotional well-being and the place of individuality in the chain of enormous organisations, companies and structures. Schumacher suggested that the annihilation of the individual in the globalised though efficient world is a recipe for a world devoid of creativity, innovation, freedom and intuition. Kumar then tackles the ecology of scale, denouncing the unjust and unsustainable ecological footprint of societies based on large-scale mass production and mass consumption. Capital has been devouring all other elements of the economy, turning our societies into disconnected and dysfunctional entities. Kumar is clear that 'this primacy of money in the economic model is the cause of the environmental crisis'.

His last scale is that of spirituality. Schumacher believed we are so clever that we could survive, for a while, without wisdom; however, at the end of the day, the 'problem of spiritual and moral truth moves into the central position'. Large economic institutions are not concerned with 'spiritual, social and environmental well-being' and so this is another challenge for our

increasing obsession with growth and the globalisation of everything. Kumar's main message in relation to Schumacher's work
is that the competition between money, natural resources and
human well-being is distorted and we need to pay more attention
to the last two and less to the first.

Usually ladies are first, but in this case Marina Silva closes with
a look at the newest of our classics, *Our Common Future*. For five
years Minister of the Environment in Brazil, Marina Silva was
a green presidential candidate in the 2010 election, achieving
an impressive third place with 20% of the votes. She is known
nationally and internationally for her fight for ethics, the preservation of natural resources and sustainable development. In 2007,
The Guardian newspaper nominated her as one of the 50 people
who could save the planet. Marina Silva wrote the essay on the
Brundtland Report, a book that helped her as a politician to define
and structure Brazil's sustainable development strategy.

Our Common Future was commissioned by the United Nations
from a group of 23 members, headed by Gro Harlem Brundtland,
who was then Prime Minister of Norway and a former Minister
for Environmental Affairs. This classic, which is also known as
the Brundtland Report, was three years in the making. However,
the effort of hundreds of collaborators was well worthwhile,
because this book not only revolutionised our understanding of
the environmental crisis but also created different perspectives
on the relationship between environmental questions and social
and economic issues. As Marina Silva says, 'according to *Our
Common Future,* the environmental crisis is essentially a crisis
of civilisation'.

This last essay begins by explaining the conceptualisation of
this demanding report and how it led to the concept of sustainable
development, based on four important dimensions: environmental, economic, social and cultural. Marina Silva realises we have
been losing ground on most of these dimensions and how hard
the road ahead will be. She also proposes further dimensions to

this equation: those of aesthetic, political and ethical sustainability. These resonate with the previous books and essays and form a very personal understanding of the challenges ahead. Unfortunately most politicians do not have the holistic perspective of Marina Silva, who defends the intrinsic value of nature and the absolute need for more ethics in the decision-making processes. As she explains with regard to the environment: 'problems seem to have no solution, not because of the lack of technical expertise or unsuitable proposals, but rather because we lack ethics'. Silva then goes on to expose the current unsuitability of the logic of political systems for creating more sustainable, inclusive, participatory and long-term policies, instead of the present short-term mentality associated with the power struggle for a career rather than seeing the concept of politics as a public forum.

Silva urges a 'more thorough questioning that focuses more on values. Here it is clear that the inappropriate way of doing comes from the inappropriate way of being'. As long as well-being is connected with material consumption, we are going nowhere, and so she proposes that 'sustainability requires from us a type of creative de-adaptation', which remains a challenge to our overly settled and spoiled establishment. Reconnecting with being rather than with having, making, owning and dominating is Silva's recipe for a more sustainable world, and with that she summarises much of the essence of the books given fresh life in this series.

'To weigh and consider'

Reading the classics reminds us of the messages and the narrative of writers whose ideas have been valued for decades, even centuries. Such works provide us with a sense of perspective for our current age and the need for a renewed awakening of our ability to question, to think, to reflect. They are enduring only so long as we continue to read them. That is the objective of this book: to provide not only new and timely interpretations of what has been written, but essentially as an appetiser for continued re-reading, which is the only way to maintain their strength as classics.

Walden stands for both learning from nature and the novelty of returning to natural settings; however, *Walden*, without the umbilical cord of continued commentary, would have been silent. *A Sand County Almanac* reminds us that protecting and nurturing natural capital is a means of building the basis for social capital, and that both have to be strong and resilient if financial capital is to offer reliable prosperity. This is the reverse of the present capitalist dilemma and the basis of the danger of present efforts to hold the Eurozone together. Maintaining the currency at the expense of workable democracy cannot succeed. And to do so without taking into account natural capital guidelines and boundaries is bound to fail. This is also the message of Schumacher, Brundtland and Meadows. There can be prosperity, but only with a wholesale redefinition of the purposes of the economy and of society.

We have to ask why Schumacher was ignored and Meadows vilified. The power brokers simply did not understand Schumacher. Brundtland is in danger of disintegrating in the face of recession and austerity for the same reasons that Leopold was misunderstood. And Meadows *et al.* threatened the world with limits, and limits are not part of the essential human condition. Carson brought the message home, but only because there was a scientific alternative to her poisoned products. As was the case with CFCs, substitutes were relatively easily found, and capitalism was left untroubled. Yet her and our failure to complete the message continues to give us other dangerous environmental problems. The fundamentals of persistent and ecosystem-damaging products, made artificially for artificial reasons, remain in place and in process.

We need to revisit these books in order to obtain inspiration for the difficult times ahead. Their strength is essentially found in their philosophical dimension and, even though the road is still long, this is a dimension we should never forget. Each book suggested a shift from an ontology dominated by narrow anthropocentric interests towards a more holistic notion of highly interdependent natural and socio-political systems. In one way or another, they all took the stance that philosophy and ethics must become a central issue in our assessments of the world. If Thoreau was a philosopher turned naturalist, Leopold was a naturalist turned philosopher. Rachel Carson was a biologist convinced of the need for justice towards nature and Schumacher was an economist who thought like a philosopher. *The Limits to Growth* and *Our Common Future* are technological and political books but they are laced with a strong philosophy of respect for nature.

As another of Calvino's definitions said:

> The classics are those books which constitute a treasured experience for those who have read and loved them; but they remain just as rich an experience for those who reserve the chance to read them for when they are in the best condition to enjoy them.

So, dear reader, if you fall into the second category, the essays that follow will certainly inspire you to enjoy *Walden, or A Sand County Almanac,* or *Silent Spring,* or *The Limits to Growth,* or *Small is Beautiful* or *Our Common Future* one of these days. If you belong to the first group, then the essays may also inspire you to revisit those books and enjoy the precious experience of rediscovery; in the words of Calvino, 'A classic is a book which with each rereading offers as much a sense of discovery as the first reading.'

We desperately need more and more people to read them and make them their own classic: 'your classic is a book to which you cannot remain indifferent, and which helps you define yourself in relation or even in opposition to it'. This is particularly urgent because what emerges from these essays is the stark conclusion that the message in all six books is clearly not being heeded. They all contain ultimate environmental truths and human challenges. And they are all classics. Yet their words continue to be ignored. Why this is so must surely be their ultimate message.

1

Walden
A tale on the 'art of living'

Viriato Soromenho-Marques

Henry David Thoreau (1817–62) and his masterpiece, *Walden*, are both ingrained in our lives. Nowadays, it is almost impossible to undertake a candid analysis of the book named after a beautiful lake, near Concord, Massachusetts, without hearing a contemporary echo of the constellation of fears that haunts us. We are the fragile inhabitants of the grim and probably desperate 'Anthropocene era'.[7] How can we accompany the thoughts and steps of Emerson's solitary friend and disciple without seeing him as a forefather of our anguish regarding the future, seemingly held prisoner by the shadows of economic doom and environmental collapse?

The author and the book

Thoreau is both a writer and a cultural legend, a giant of American literature and a hero for those who praise typical American individualism, albeit of the milder, more elaborate and intellectually oriented New England type. During his lifetime, Thoreau lived within the sphere of attraction of the great founder of the so-called American transcendentalist movement, Ralph Waldo Emerson. He shared the ideas and ideals of that spiritual stream that boasted an alien German, or even Prussian resonance, and which stemmed from the philosophical works of Immanuel Kant (1724–1804). However, the gulf between Emerson and Kant is much wider than the apparent identity derived from the 'transcendental' concept. Thoreau was just one of Emerson's followers and companions, much like Margaret Fuller, Amos Bronson Alcott, George Ripley and Theodore Parker. Nevertheless, we can clearly see that he was too intensively engaged in the process of personal knowledge and self-transformation to worry about fame or economic and social rewards, or even his place in American literary history.

Thoreau was neither a prolific writer nor a bestselling author; even his masterpiece was far from being a literary success. The basis for *Walden*'s lasting influence lies deep in the collective American psyche. In a sense, Thoreau, alongside Whitman, constructed the two forms of 19th-century American soul. The latter was able to listen to the songs and aspirations of millions of men and women, struggling to achieve their dreams in a new, vibrant and labouring nation, while the former was a walking philosophical manifesto for the courage of trying to explore the maze of the inner conscience, and the hidden grounds of moral judgement.[8] *Walden* is the testimony of a life seeking the unity of idea and action, of values and deeds. The reason why we consider this book a pioneering classic within the already vast canon of environmental literature is related to the fact that, for Thoreau, as well for Emerson, there is no truly ontological barrier between human-kind and nature. They are both modalities of thought. Becoming a true moral human being is the path that leads us to the understanding that ultimately, instead of a chasm between things and ideas, it is the unity of natural beauty and moral good that will prevail. For Thoreau, humans are the creatures that are able to find themselves while looking for nature; or the beings that, when in silent meditation, achieve the clear notion that trees, birds, sunlight, running water, the shifting seasons, nature as a whole is a core element of our own identity. Nature is not only our home, but also the best part of ourselves.[9]

Walden was published in 1854, in Boston, by Ticknor & Fields. It was not Thoreau's first literary outing and he already had a few titles to his name. His first attempt at the contemplation of nature and philosophical appraisal appeared in 1849: *A Week on the Concord and Merrimack Rivers*. In the same year, he published the short essay that would put him on the shortlist of major Western political philosophers: *Civil Disobedience*. *Walden* saw the light of day in the same year as an essay on the contentious topic that would force the USA onto the bloody battlefields of civil war: *Slavery in Massachusetts* (1854). This would be followed by an essay on the controversy surrounding a hero who was executed as a criminal: *A Plea for Captain John Brown* (1859).

The world of *Walden*

On 4 July 1845, when Thoreau left Concord on the way to his new dwelling, a wood cabin by one of the finest natural relics of the last Ice Age in Massachusetts, the Walden Pond, he was not overly distressed, but probably looking forward hopefully to the outcome of a rather difficult decision. For him, going to live in the wild meant doing away with the ancient institution that enslaves the human race in a kind of ethical minor age: the gap between values and deeds:

> I went to the woods because I wished to live deliberately, to front only the essential facts of life, and see if I could not learn what it had to teach, and not, when I came to die, discover that I had not lived . . . I wanted to live deep and suck out all the marrow of life.[10]

The young and practical philosopher was ready to live according to his own beliefs. He was very much aware of the rapidly shifting world around him. America was already at the centre of this movement. He could not know that world population growth, which constituted an increasing threat to nature, anticipated by Robert Malthus in 1798, would reach the staggering figure of about 1,260 million by the end of the 1840s. However, he probably knew about the exponential increase in the American population, which leapt 35.9%, from 17,069,453 inhabitants in 1840 to 23,191,876 in 1850.[11] He knew from experience the harm humans were capable of doing to beautiful landscapes. The waves of immigrants coming from Europe in search of a dream came close to the shores of Walden. From the woodchoppers to the expanding railroad, from the Irish raising pigs by the water to the ice-men in winter, the outcome of the meeting between newcomers and the pond was far from ideal.[12]

Long before his journey to Walden Pond, Thoreau underwent a kind of profound and silent academic and literary preparation. Modern readers cannot help being struck by the encyclopaedic knowledge that jumps from the pages of his literary masterpiece. Modern-day universities do not provide students with anywhere near the bountiful information and wisdom that Thoreau received during his school years at Harvard University, between 1833 and 1837. Reading Thoreau, we encounter a vivid example of the blending of humanities and natural sciences, before the definitive arrival of the great 'two cultures' divide.[13] Having mastered both classical languages and quantitative methodology, he was able to combine Homer with empirical data from natural sciences, as well as acute quantitative remarks with elaborate moral reflection, drawing upon classical moral philosophers.

En route to his calm and pleasant destination, Thoreau was well aware that the world he was living in was in the throes of a rapid and breath-taking shift. The huge impact of an industrial revolution was quickly spreading from its small British source. Huge urban areas were swallowing up millions of peasants and large areas of forest and farmland. Acid smog was taking the place of mild fog in the vicinity of cities. Speed was everywhere, demanding more tasks in less time, and in the way people talked, thought, or moved from one place to another. Nevertheless, reading Thoreau, we can confirm that the world where Walden Pond was located was less important to the writer than the world he wanted to build in his inner house by the lake—a house that was not the humble cabin where he slept at night, but rather his deeper moral self. The sounds and shades of the forest gave him the space he needed for the personal pursuit of his own identity. As such, Walden was not the final destination, but a geographical condition for a deeper psychological journey. Thoreau was entirely in agreement with his mentor, Ralph Waldo Emerson, when the latter critically targeted the urban condition for its major spiritual shortcomings: 'Cities give not the human senses room enough. We go out daily and nightly to feed the eyes on the horizon, and require so much scope, just as we need water for our bath.'[14]

The world in *Walden*

The cornerstone of Thoreau's worldview is personal autonomy: to be what we are, or what we may become, regardless of what other people say about us. Worse still, we need to shed prejudices about ourselves, formulated when we assimilate an estranged view about our own personal endeavours: 'Public opinion is a weak tyrant compared with our own private opinion.'[15] Self-inflicted tyranny is just part of the riddle in which personal autonomy becomes just a hollow phrase. Another crucial issue that affects the clarity of our moral vision is the wrong hierarchy of values: 'I see young men, my townsmen, whose misfortune is to have inherited farms, houses, barns, cattle, and farming tools; for these are more easily acquired than got rid of . . . Who made them serfs of the soil?'[16] Instead of *being,* we chose *having.* It is so easy to neglect the duties towards our own self when it seems possible to find an easier nest in the glamour of material wealth and in the approval of a shallow public mind. Nevertheless, the bottom line lies in the hardship of the path toward actual ethical grandeur. Thoreau reminds his readers, bluntly: 'While civilization has been improving our houses, it has not equally improved the men who are to inhabit them. It has created palaces, but it was not so easy to create noblemen and kings.'[17]

It is no wonder that, alongside the founder of American transcendentalism, Ralph Waldo Emerson, Thoreau is considered as a kind of New World pioneer of 20th-century continental European existential philosophy, which has its roots in 19th-century thinkers such as Nietzsche and Kierkegaard. For Thoreau, much like Nietzsche, the nature of philosophical truth is not a matter of logical coherence and linguistic order, but rather a question of practical courage. In his sober and imperative style, Nietzsche asked himself and his readers: 'How much truth can a spirit carry upon its shoulders, how much truth can a spirit dare to bear? For me, those have been more and more the real measure of value.'[18] Thoreau could be considered a living example of the courage involved in the pursuit of truth against all odds. The great challenge is the ability to live at the same level as such praised and chosen ideals:

> There are nowadays professors of philosophy, but not
> philosophers ... To be a philosopher is not merely to
> have subtle thoughts, nor even to found a school, but so
> to love wisdom as to live according to its dictates, a life
> of simplicity, independence, magnanimity, and trust.[19]

The road to becoming an authentic person is hard and painful. The modern world created a huge maze of noisy objects that disturb our capacity to remain faithful to the basic principles of personal integrity. Without knowing, Thoreau was challenging the Protestant work ethic, much as a young contemporary called Karl Marx did in 1844. They both wrote about a kind of work that deprives the labourer of his own psychological identity:

> Actually, the laboring man has not leisure for a true
> integrity day by day; he cannot afford to sustain the
> manliest relations to men; his labor would be depreci-
> ated in the market. He has no time to be any thing but
> a machine.[20]

Thoreau was also keen to show the process by which technology was able to dominate our lives, instead of serving human ends: 'We do not ride on the railroad; it rides upon us.'[21] However, contrary to Marx, Thoreau did not believe that salvation from the 'factory system' would be a social and political revolution, grounded on a global theory of history and on a systemic understanding of capitalism as a 'mode of production'. Still in the domain of work and production, Thoreau asked his permanent fundamental question: what can I do? Once more, ethics was the key to liberation. Social emancipation should start with the individual's capacity to set his own agenda, his mastering of time and occupation:

> I found, that by working about six weeks in a year, I
> could meet all the expenses of living ... In short, I am
> convinced, both by faith and experience, that to main-
> tain one's self on this earth is not a hardship but a pas-
> time, if we will live simply and wisely; as the pursuits
> of the simpler nations are still the sports of the more
> artificial.[22]

Pristine nature is the place where the roots of ethical judgement can best find their way to the human soul. However, the
issue of ethics leads us to the need to make decisions regarding
others in a shared and noisy world, the basis of which goes deep
into the silent realm of personal identity. The society of landscapes and natural creatures is the most suitable nourishment for
self-knowledge. Solitude is a pre-condition for virtue:

> I love to be alone. I never found the companion that was
> so companionable as solitude . . . Society is commonly
> too cheap. We meet at very short intervals, not having
> had time to acquire any new value for each other.[23]

Thoreau has a good understanding of how humans can have a negative impact on nature. However, he tends to emphasise nature's
resilience, bringing together the regenerative strength of natural
cycles and the remembrance of his youthful reverence towards a
world in the never-ending process of revelation.

> Though the woodchoppers have laid bare first this shore
> and then that, and the Irish have built their sties by it,
> and the railroad has infringed on its border, and the
> ice-men have skimmed it once, it is itself unchanged,
> the same water which my youthful eyes fell on; all the
> change is in me.[24]

Nature works for Thoreau as a kind of ethical *topos*. From nature
flows the power that is able to enhance personal development,
and moral autonomy. Humans are, therefore, very interested in
nature. However, Thoreau strictly follows Emerson's teachings
regarding the need to distinguish sheer pragmatic and material
interest from the involvement in nature for spiritual and ontological reasons.[25] Walking along the shores of Walden, feeling
the languid texture of time, using the lenses of leisure for sharp
natural observations, Thoreau revered the diversity and plenty of
nature, and used it as a blueprint for a human commonwealth,
vibrant with people, eager to absorb and develop their uniqueness and individuality:

I desire that there may be as many different persons in
the world as possible, but I would have each one be very
careful to find out and pursue *his own way*, and not his
father's or his mother's or his neighbor's instead.[26]

The politics of *Walden*

The same man who was able to live alone in a humble cabin by
the water, listening to the signs and noises of an expanding Concord at a distance, was the same person who was about to gain the
enduring status of a cosmopolitan hero in the fight for political
justice and civic fairness within modern republican politics. For
Thoreau, there is no contradiction between the fierce pursuit of
self-knowledge and moral autonomy in the universe of personal
singularity, on one hand, and the need to create the political
fabric on solid foundation, based on the rule of law and mutual
respect, on the other. Individualism and republicanism belong to
the same sphere of concern and action: the never-ending struggle
for a better world, either within the reaches of the inner soul, or
in the wider realm of the outer world.

As in the quest for natural contemplation, for Thoreau, the case
for political justice also began at his own doorstep, in the heart of
his home town, in his native state and everywhere in his beloved
America. The short essay on the concept and praxis of civil disobedience, published five years before *Walden*, is a strong statement against the way America was severing the links with the
best of its own political tradition. The former beacon of liberty,
beaming a hopeful light through the darkness of a cruel world
of tyranny and suffering, was drifting away from its principles
and towards sheer economic growth and brutal territorial expansion. The essay, written in 1849, will forever stand as a land-
mark in terms of the method for shifting from ethical reflection

to blunt political grounds, in a transition that is able to overcome any resistance and opposition placing itself on a superior level of reasoning: a single man against the overwhelming majority of his nation and the universal trends of his time—that was the fight chosen by Thoreau when he refused to pay taxes to a country that was waging war against both human dignity and international law. Vindicating American slaves and Mexicans, Thoreau was prepared to start his own personal revolution:

> When a sixth of the population of a nation which has undertaken to be the refuge of liberty are slaves and a whole country is unjustly overrun and conquered by a foreign army, and subjected to the military law, I think that it is not too soon for honest men to rebel and revolutionize.[27]

Justice has everything to do with coherence. In nature, beauty is the sign of a perfect matching of parts in a landscape aiming for a certain kind of completeness; justice is society's surrogate for beauty. Every polity shall look towards harmony, in the distribution of social and politically common goods. Liberty cannot be the preserve of some citizens, and the desperate, distant dream of so many others. It is easy to acknowledge the way he masters the contradiction between America's promises and the harsh realities of the time. However, the core of Thoreau's argument does not belong to history, but rather to the merging of ethics and politics. In a truly Kantian insight, Thoreau affirms the identity between the moral subject and the concerned citizen. They both identify the profound abyss between the inner core of societies and individuals: an abyss between good and evil. Only 'action from principle' will allow the former to prevail over the latter:

> Action from principle, the perception and the performance of right, changes things and relations; it is essentially revolutionary, and does not consist wholly with anything which was. It not only divides states and churches, it divides family; ay, it divides the *individual*, separating the diabolical in him from the divine.[28]

There is an almost linear continuity between the role of individuals in the moral voyage undertaken in *Walden*, and the tasks individual citizens have to perform within the boundaries of society. In both situations, the key lies not in quantitative majorities, but in the fact of being right or wrong. Thoreau introduces the formidable concept of 'a majority of one' as a revolutionary strength based upon moral righteousness.[29] Therefore, we may also look towards history, using respect for individual rights as a parameter of evaluation, as a kind of indicator of progress; according to Thoreau, that is the true essence of a meaningful reading of apparently contradictory events throughout universal history. Much better than technical achievements, moral and legal improvements can establish a philosophical metric for the history of humankind:

> The progress from an absolute to a limited monarchy, from a limited monarchy to a democracy, is a progress toward a true respect for the individual . . . Is a democracy, such as we know it, the last improvement possible in government? Is it not possible to take a step further towards recognizing and organizing the rights of man?[30]

The 'Art of Living' and *Walden*'s legacy

It is almost impossible to gauge the full historical impact of *Walden*. Several generations later, the book still belongs to both academic and popular culture. It helps us to understand the way American environmental public policy began and developed, as well as being a common gift given to children by parents worried about the transition from childhood to the turbulent challenges and ordeals of youth. It is difficult to find a single American public figure in the annals of environmental policy that was not moved by the sunsets Thoreau experienced near Walden Pond.

Two years after his passing, George Perkins Marsh published his pioneering *Man and Nature* (1864). John Muir, President Theodore Roosevelt, Gifford Pinchot (President of the US Forest Service during the Theodore Roosevelt years), Harold Ickes (who managed the US National Park Service during F.D. Roosevelt's presidencies), Aldo Leopold, Rachel Carson, Kenneth Boulding—all these prominent personalities owe an intellectual debt to the author of *Walden*. From the extraordinary Forest Reserve Act (1891), drawn up in a rare benign gesture from Congress to the conservation efforts of three different presidents (Benjamin Harrison, Grover Cleveland and William McKinley), to the expansion of nature reserves during Theodore Roosevelt's presidencies and modern dreams and adventures, like the pilgrimage of young Christopher McCandless, with its tragic ending, depicted in Sean Penn's famous movie *Into the Wild* (2007), Thoreau's profound and widespread cultural influence never ceases to surprise.[31]

The influence of *Walden* can also be found in other classic environmental literature, which is dealt with in other chapters in this book. At different literary levels and narrative places, it is impossible to ignore the living shadow and footprints of Thoreau's pilgrimage around the shores of his beloved lake in the other acute contemplation of nature depicted in the pages of *A Sand County Almanac*, by Aldo Leopold, or in the quest for knowledge and wisdom developed by Rachel Carson in her surprising and politically influential *Silent Spring*.[32]

I believe, however, that the most essential source of strength, which even the contemporary reader can sense in the pages of *Walden*, lies in his militant involvement with the idea of life as both an ethical and aesthetical endeavour, reminiscent of the 'Art of Living'. The concept of the 'Art of living' appeared in John Stuart Mill's *Principles of Political Economy*, in 1848, almost at the same time Thoreau was leaving Walden to return to modern urban life. Mill spoke about the virtually boundless spiritual and cultural progress and development contained in the notion

of the 'Art of living', establishing a sharp contrast with the necessary physical limits for material growth, within the framework of
his proposal for the economic stationary state, probably one of
the most elaborate pioneering bases of any modern sustainability
theory.[33]

For Thoreau, the future concept of sustainability would not be
an end in itself, but rather the condition for personal freedom.
Respect for nature, the moderate use of natural resources and an
acute awareness of signs of decline in natural systems were all
behaviours connected to the capacity of self-listening that only
solitude can bring. Only through the severe test of loneliness
could one hope for the possibility of a society made up of strong
and free individuals. Only those able to take care of themselves
would be able to cherish and care for our planet. Only those
who dare to dream of and act for a better world will inherit the
Earth.[34]

2

A Sand County Almanac
An evolutionary-ecological worldview

J. Baird Callicott

About the author

First a word about the author of *A Sand County Almanac*. Aldo Leopold was born on 11 January 1887 into a prosperous, public-spirited commercial family of German descent—keenly interested in the natural sciences and the fine and liberal arts—in Burlington, Iowa, a Mississippi River town. As a boy, he showed an avid interest in natural history, especially bird watching, and an enthusiasm for hunting. His father, Carl, an impassioned hunter himself, imparted to his sons both extraordinary hunting skills and ethical restraints in the pursuit of game. The teenaged Leopold was sent to the elite Lawrenceville School in New Jersey, which prepared him for matriculation into Yale University, where, after five years, he was graduated from the Yale Forest School with a master's degree, in 1909. That year he joined the US Forest Service and was posted to the Southwest Territories—then they had not yet become states—of Arizona and New Mexico.[35]

Leopold steadily rose in the ranks of the Service, but was less interested its principal remit, timber production, than with the 'thrifty' condition of the forest itself.[36] As he would later characterise it, he was interested in the 'beauty' of the national forest lands as well as their 'utility'.[37] He was, accordingly, alarmed at soil erosion, caused by livestock grazing and fire suppression; and he was interested in the animals inhabiting the national forests— only in part because he was an ardent hunter. In his wide-ranging Forest Service fieldwork, Leopold also developed a love for roadless travel by horse, pack train and canoe. Consistent with all these concerns and interests, he was among the first civil servants to propose a system of wilderness reserves in the US National Forests.[38]

In 1924, Leopold was posted to the Forest Products Laboratory in Madison, Wisconsin. He was not happy in that post and resigned from the Service in 1928 to become a consultant to the Sporting Arms and Ammunition Manufacturers' Institute, conducting game surveys and overseeing wildlife research in the Midwestern states. Leopold was barely able to support his wife and five children during the ensuing Great Depression, but used the involuntary leisure it afforded him to write a field-defining text, *Game Management*, published in 1933. That book led to an appointment at the University of Wisconsin as Professor of Game Management in the Department of Agricultural Economics. He remained a college professor for the rest of his life, eventually heading his own Department of Wildlife Management (later to become the Department of Wildlife Ecology). From that position he assumed a leadership role in the American conservation movement. He was among the founders of the Wilderness Society and the Wildlife Society and he served the Ecological Society of America as president, among other similar organisational offices and services.[39]

In 1935, Leopold bought 80 acres (~40 hectares) of exhausted farmland on the Wisconsin River, some 50 miles (~80 kilometres) north of Madison, which he planned to use for waterfowl hunting. The farmhouse had burned down and the only standing building was a chicken coop or cowshed full of manure. Leopold and his family converted that building into a camp cabin—adding a bunk-room, fireplace and chimney—that they dubbed 'the shack'. They soon turned to the task of planting pine trees and prairie vegeta-tion. Although the concept had not been fully articulated by then, theirs was among the first projects of ecological restoration.

About the book

In the early 1940s, at the behest of the New York publisher, Alfred A. Knopf, Leopold began work, in a desultory way, on a book of nature essays. The publisher asked him to write 'a personal book recounting adventures in the field . . . warmly, evocatively, and vividly written . . . a book for the layman . . . [with] room for the author's opinions on ecology and conservation . . . worked into a framework of actual field experience'.[40] Leopold's plan was to include some very argumentative pieces that he had already written and published in various outlets during the 1930s, along with some more descriptive, less judgemental pieces that he was writing for *The Wisconsin Agriculturist and Farmer*. Despite the initial provision of 'room for the author's opinions on ecology and conservation', the editors at Knopf found that kind of essay to be repetitive and tedious. They decided that what they really wanted was 'a book purely of nature observations'.[41] Further, they found Leopold's essays to be scattered not only in subject mat-ter, but also in place (from the Southwest to the Midwest, from Canada to Mexico) and time (from Leopold's boyhood to his early days in the forest service to his latter days as a college professor). Leopold's essays, therefore, lacked the classic Aristotelian uni-ties of time and place, which characterised nature-writing genre exemplars, such as *Walden; or Life in the Woods* by Henry David Thoreau, and *The Outermost House: A Year on the Great Beach of Cape Cod* by Henry Beston. His essays also varied radically in length—'Draba', for example, filling only half a page, 'Good Oak' twelve pages.

In response to these criticisms, Leopold struggled throughout the decade to produce a book that had all the qualities that Knopf first suggested: a book that was personal, addressed to a broad lay audience, and opinionated—all worked into a framework of actual field experience. He declined to write a book of 'mere natural history' (as he styled it), a book 'purely of nature observations' (as they did).[42] And so Knopf declined to publish the manuscript as submitted in 1947. It was also rejected by Macmillan and the University of Minnesota Press. Bitterly disappointed, Leopold discarded the more conventional Foreword he had written by way of an introduction in July 1947 and replaced it with a new, pithier Foreword written in March 1948. He then relinquished the task of finding a publisher to his son, Luna, who sent it to William Sloan Associates and to Oxford University Press. Oxford immediately accepted it for publication without critical comment or demand for extensive revision. Trouble in getting published the book on which he had worked so hard was not the only trouble plaguing his life at that time. He was suffering from 'tic douloureaux' (trigeminal neuralgia), an excruciatingly painful irritation of a facial nerve, and vehement political opposition to his management plan for reducing the size of the deer herd in northern Wisconsin. Just a week after receiving the good news from OUP, Leopold died—pleased at least by this long-awaited happy outcome—at age 61, on 21 April 1948.[43]

Because Luna Leopold had already taken a substantial role in getting his father's manuscript accepted for publication, he guided it through the production process. He proceeded on the principle that the eventual book should be as faithful as possible to the volume that his father had crafted. Leopold's own title, *Great Possessions*, was, however, wisely discarded. He had titled the first and longest of the three parts of the book 'A Sauk County Almanac', because 'the shack' and its environs, the setting of Part I, were located in Sauk County, Wisconsin (named for the Indian tribe that had once lived there). No one now knows who suggested that 'Sauk County' be changed to 'Sand County'— but, whoever deserves the credit, it was stroke of genius. There is no Sand County, Wisconsin, but the shack and its environs were located in the sandy outwash plain of the glacier that covered half the state from the northwest to the southeast as recently as 12,000 years ago. The region was (and is) known in Wisconsin as 'the sand counties' or 'the central sands'. And so the book was published in 1949 as *A Sand County Almanac and Sketches Here and There*.[44]

For Knopf and the other publishers who had rejected Leopold's manuscript, the main issue could be boiled down to one thing: 'unity'. And upon first encounter, the book does appear to be a hodgepodge of variegated materials.

Part I shifts from casually following a skunk track in the first essay; to making firewood from a lightning-killed oak, in the second (all the while providing an environmental history of the ground in which it was rooted); to migrating geese in the third; then on to loving descriptions of various humble plants (such as draba) and animals (such as woodcock); to episodes of fishing and hunting; to activities of ecological restoration, such as tree planting and culling. To mute the jarring effect of their disparate subject matter, Leopold obligingly supplied the essays of Part I, but only of Part I, with the Aristotelian unities of time and place. They are organised by the months of the calendar year; and the place in which they are set is the shack landscape—Leopold's Waldenesque 'week-end refuge from too much modernity'. (In the 'Foreword', Leopold informally refers to Part I as the 'shack sketches'.[45])

Part II, 'Sketches Here and There', gently transitions from the well-circumscribed shack environs to Wisconsin at large. Then the setting of the essays shifts a little farther away to the neighbouring states of Illinois and Iowa; then it jumps to the more distant American Southwest (Arizona and New Mexico); then turns sharply south to Chihuahua and Sonora in Mexico; then moves back north to Oregon and Utah and finally to Manitoba in Canada. Sketches here and there indeed!—all loosely organised by state or province and scattered across the whole North American continent. And, again, the subject matter ranges just as widely in Part II as it does in Part I: from threatened cranes to the extinct passenger pigeon to canoeing on a river in 'Wisconsin'; from a bus journey through cornfields to a brutal youthful hunting vignette in 'Illinois and Iowa'; from climbing mountains to exterminating bears and wolves in 'Arizona and New Mexico'; from parrots to the delta of the Colorado River and a mountain stream in 'Chihuahua and Sonora'; from an invasive species of grass in 'Oregon and Utah' to a lonely, wild marsh in 'Manitoba'.

Part III, 'The Upshot', totally abandons any attempt to supply a transparent literary device of unification. It consists of four longer 'philosophical' essays, the first two of which are strident rebukes of unethical hunting practices, while the third is a poignant appeal for wilderness preservation. The fourth is 'The Land Ethic', which Leopold himself had placed first in the final section, but was moved (again wisely) to the climactic conclusion of Part III and of the book as a whole.

Were the editors at Knopf right to complain that the manuscript Leopold submitted lacked unity? Leopold thought not. He had taken their criticisms to heart and worked to overcome their concerns and replied of his submitted essays: 'I still think that they have a unity as they are.'[46] The book has become a classic of conservation philosophy, the bible of the contemporary environmental movement. Translated into a dozen languages, it has universal appeal. Evidently in *A Sand County Almanac* as in the

United States of America, *e pluribus unum*—from many one. But what is its principle of unity, what makes of that variegated many a unified whole? There is one underlying, persistent, thematic thread that Leopold weaves through the fabric of his masterpiece from the first pages to the last: the exposition and promulgation of an evolutionary-ecological worldview and its axiological (ethical and aesthetical) and normative (practical moral) implications. Leopold's bold project in *A Sand County Almanac* is nothing short of worldview remediation. And, whether consciously or not, I think that his prospective publishers sensed that and reacted negatively—not to the book's lack of unity, but to its very radical and revolutionary unifying theme. They were afraid that the book-buying public would be offended:

> What we like best is the nature observations, and the more objective narratives and essays. We like less the subjective parts—that is, the philosophical reflections which are less fresh and which one reader finds sometimes 'fatuous'. The ecological argument almost everyone finds unconvincing.[47]

Leopold's was an unsettling book, an affront to post-war blue-skies optimism and self-satisfaction.

The argument of the Foreword: toward worldview remediation

Leopold plainly and guilelessly announces the nature of his project in the 'Foreword', but with such charm and indirection that the enormous scope and scale of it might easily be missed: 'Conservation is getting nowhere,' he writes, 'because it is incompatible with our Abrahamic *concept* of land.'[48] One of Leopold's favourite rhetorical devices is synecdoche, letting the part stand for the whole.[49] Our Abrahamic concept of land is, more forthrightly put, our inherited biblical worldview. In accordance with that worldview, Leopold claims, 'We abuse land because we regard it as a commodity belonging to us.'[50] Toward the end of the book, in 'The Land Ethic', Leopold evokes the same synecdoche for the biblical worldview once more: 'Abraham knew what the land was for: it was to drip milk and honey into Abraham's mouth. At the present moment, the assurance with which we regard this assumption is inverse to our education.'[51]

Leopold here anticipates the (in)famous environmental critique of the biblical worldview by historian Lynn White Jr at the zenith of public awareness of and concern about an 'environmental crisis'. White laid ultimate blame for what he called 'the ecologic crisis' on the biblical ideas that 'man' is created in the 'image of God', given 'dominion' over the rest of creation, and charged to 'subdue' it.[52] Whether Leopold and White correctly understand the particulars of the biblical worldview or how it has shaped Christendom's cultural attitudes toward the natural world is another question, which has been much debated. My present point is that Leopold *thought* that the biblical worldview is incompatible with conservation. Grafted on to the biblical foundations of the 20th-century Western worldview was the emergence—following World War II—of mass consumerism:

> our bigger and better society is now like a hypochondriac, so obsessed with its own economic health as to have lost the capacity to remain healthy. The whole world is so greedy for more bathtubs [another synecdoche] that it has lost the stability necessary to build them or even to turn off the tap.[53]

Rather than accommodate conservation to that toxic mix of biblical dominionism and mass consumerism, Leopold instead proposed to replace it with a more coherent and comprehensive alternative: 'I suppose it may be said that these essays tell the company how it may get back in step.'[54] Thoreau, as everyone knows, claimed to step to the beat of a 'different drummer' and was proud to be out of step with the company—19th-century American cultural attitudes and values.[55] Leopold boldly insists that the company—20th-century Western civilization—get in step with the better beat of the drummer to which he had learned to march. 'When we see land as a community to which we belong,' Leopold continues, 'we may begin to use it with love and respect ... That land is a community is the basic concept of ecology, but that land is to be loved and respected is an extension of ethics. That land yields a cultural harvest is a fact long known but latterly often forgotten.'[56]

To repeat, my central claim is this: *A Sand County Almanac*, at first blush a mere hodgepodge of charming but disparate vignettes, has a single overarching and unifying theme and purpose—the exposition and promulgation of an evolutionary-ecological worldview and its axiological and normative implications. 'These essays,' Leopold goes on, 'attempt to weld these three concepts'—the community-concept of ecology, ethics and aesthetics (the cultural harvest yielded by land).[57]

The argument in Part I: the inter-subjective biotic community

'Nothing could be more salutary,' Leopold concludes in the Foreword, 'than a little healthy contempt for a plethora of material blessings. Perhaps such a *shift of values* can be achieved by reappraising things unnatural, tame, and confined in terms of things natural, wild, and free.' Turn the page, and Leopold's effort to induce a culture-wide 'shift of values'—a wholesale paradigm shift—begins right on the downbeat.[58] The first (and only) essay in 'January', the first section of Part I, 'the shack sketches', is 'January Thaw'. The author is awakened by dripping water and goes outside to see what's up. He follows a skunk track 'curious *to deduce* his *state of mind and appetite*, and destination if any'.[59] The ecologist, like a natural-history version of Sherlock Holmes, deduces hidden facts from clues. To be an ecologist is a mind-challenging, adventurous occupation. (And we readers secretly want to be Dr Watson to his Holmes—sharing in the fun of discovery, by following the lead of the masterly sleuth.) Leopold first comes upon '[a] meadow mouse, startled by my approach, [who] darts damply across the skunk track'. The eco-detective's mind starts to work: 'Why is he abroad in daylight? Probably because he *feels grieved* about the thaw.'[60] Leopold goes on gently to satirise the prevailing anthropocentrism of the Abrahamic worldview by comparing it with the microtocentrism of a mouse's worldview: 'The mouse is a sober citizen who knows that grass grows in order that mice may store it as underground haystacks, and that snow falls in order that mice may build subways from stack to stack: supply, demand, and transport all neatly organized'—but 'the thawing sun has mocked the basic premises of the microtine economic system.'[61] Just what is being mocked here and by whom?

Putting all such things in post-modern perspective, Leopold follows by treating his reader to a buteocentric worldview: The author sees

> A rough-legged hawk . . . sailing over the meadow. Now he stops, hovers like a kingfisher, and then drops like a feathered bomb into the marsh. He does not rise again, so I am sure he has caught and is now eating some worried mouse-engineer . . . The rough-legged has no opinion why grass grows, but he is well aware that snow melts in order that hawks may again catch mice.[62]

For most of Leopold's contemporaries, one unwelcome implication of the theory of evolution, of which ecology is but an extension, is that 'man' is an animal no more special or privileged in the larger scheme of things than any other animal. We humans know by the most incontrovertible evidence—introspection—that we have states of mind and appetites, feelings and passions.

To impute states of mind and appetites, feelings and passions to the other animals is therefore perfectly consistent with the evolutionary-ecological worldview. Leopold thus freely indulges in the anthropomorphic personification of other animals as central to his project of worldview remediation. The community concept— 'the basic concept of ecology'—has an interior, a subjective, as well as an exterior, objective aspect. The shack sketches are full of 'scientific natural history', as the British ecologist and Leopold's friend Charles Elton defined 'ecology'—all sorts of interesting and engaging ecological observations.[63] But Leopold also subtly works at portraying the inter-subjectivity, the interiority of the biotic community.

Leopold first blithely disregards the nearly universal scepticism about animal minds, not only evinced by those under the sway of the biblical worldview, which posits a metaphysical divide between humans and animals, but also evinced by his fellow scientists under the sway of Logical Positivism. He eventually confronts it, however, in 'The Geese Return' in the 'March' section of Part I. To do so, he begins by reinforcing his conflation of the human and animal worlds with a comparison that decidedly favours the animal:

> A March morning is only as drab as he who walks in it without a glance skyward, ear cocked for geese. I once knew a lady, *banded* by Phi Beta Kappa, who told me that she had never heard or seen the geese that twice a year proclaim the revolving seasons to her well-insulated roof. Is education possibly trading awareness for things of lesser worth? The goose who trades his is soon a pile of feathers.[64]

Leopold then goes on to pique scepticism about animal minds to the point of outrage: 'The geese that proclaim the seasons to our farm are aware of many things, including the Wisconsin statutes.'[65] That, of course, is, on the face of it, absurd. Geese may be 'aware of many things'—or they may not be—but they are not aware of the laws of the state of Wisconsin. Certainly not. But they *are* aware of the impact on human behaviour of those Wisconsin statutes governing waterfowl hunting:

> The southbound November flocks pass over us high and haughty, with scarcely a honk of recognition for their favorite sandbars and sloughs ... November geese are aware that every marsh and pond bristles from dawn till dark with hopeful guns.[66]

And we can believe that they are indeed. However, 'March geese are a different story.'

That point scored, Leopold steps up his anthropomorphic personification of geese. The gabbling geese '*debate* the merits of the day's dinner'.[67] Their gathering is a 'spring goose *convention*' whereat 'one notices the prevalence of singles—lone geese that do much flying about and much *talking*'.[68] Thus, '[o]ne is apt to impute a disconsolate tone to their honkings and to jump to the conclusion that they are broken-hearted *widowers*, or *mothers* hunting lost *children*'.[69] However, '[t]he seasoned ornithologist knows that such subjective interpretation of bird behavior is ...'[70] Leopold does not say 'unscientific' or 'unverifiable', but simply 'risky'. He then tells a tale of data-gathering by his graduate students counting 'for half a dozen years the number of geese comprising a flock', followed by 'mathematical analysis', all indicating that:

> lone geese in spring are probably just what our fond imaginings had first suggested. They are bereaved survivors of the winter's shooting, searching in vain for their kin. Now I am free to grieve with and for the lone honkers.[71]

Unstated but scarcely unnoticeable in this vignette is the background evolutionary assumption that if we are entitled confidently to impute states of mind to our fellow humans—on the basis of what we know of our own states of mind, their behaviour, and

our knowledge of human social structures—we are no less entitled confidently to impute states of mind to our fellow voyagers
in the odyssey of evolution on the basis of what we know of our
own states of mind, their behaviour, and our knowledge of their
social structures. To the Positivist complaint that we can never
directly observe the state of mind of another animal and verify
our hypotheses concerning their thoughts and feelings, Leopold
need only reply that we can never directly observe the state of
mind of another human being. The only consciousness that one
can directly observe is one's own—a somewhat unsettling realisation, enticing a few idiosyncratic sceptics to espouse solipsism.
But how can one seriously doubt that the state of mind of a person, whose face reddens, fists clench, and neck veins swell, upon
suffering an insult added to an injury, would be exactly one's own
if one were standing in their shoes. Of course, we can never be as
confident that we know other animal minds as well as we think
we know other human minds, but that they have minds and that
they share with us a full suite of basic animal appetites, passions
and feelings—hunger, thirst, sexual craving, fear and rage—is
beyond doubt, from an evolutionary-ecological point of view.

In Part I, Leopold's project of worldview remediation is
approached relentlessly, but also indirectly and subliminally.
Jumping right up on a soapbox and preaching a new gospel is
hardly ever effective. In Part I, he never refers to evolution or ecology by name. Leopold is keenly aware that his readers' wariness
must be overcome by charm and humour and that his message
must be conveyed obliquely. The voice is first-person singular,
'I'. The tense is present. The author's persona is warm, amiable,
intelligent, literate, witty, wry, ironic, entertaining and self-con-
fident. He seems only to observe and describe, to share his experience and knowledge. Yes, he gently criticises and sometimes
ridicules human foibles and follies, but never stridently or bitterly—rather, always tastefully, understatedly, and with a touch of
ironic humour.

The argument in Part II: the evolutionary aspect

In Part II, 'Sketches Here and There', the voice shifts from first-person singular to the first-person plural, to 'we', and the tense shifts from present to past. It's not about what I (the author) see and do, think and feel, but about what *we*, collectively, as a culture, believe and about how *our* prevailing attitudes and values have led *us* astray in our relationship with things natural, wild and free and how those attitudes and values must change if they are to accord with what evolutionary biology and ecology—now by name—have revealed to *us*, not only about nature but about ourselves and our place in nature.

James Brown, 'the Godfather of Soul', introduced many innovations to African-American music. Arguably his greatest was a heavy emphasis on 'The One', the first beat of every four-beat measure (as opposed to the emphasis on the second and fourth in traditional blues and jazz). Leopold was ahead of his time in this particular as in so many others. Just as the one, 'January Thaw', of Part I, gets right on the evolutionary-ecological groove, 'Marshland Elegy', the first essay in Part II, also hits that theme hard right from the downbeat.

In my opinion, 'Marshland Elegy', the first essay in Part II, 'Sketches Here and There', is the most beautiful piece in the book, from a purely literary point of view. It begins with a visual metaphor: a bank of fog covering a crane marsh as the 'white ghost of a glacier' that covered the place thousands of years ago—thus immediately evoking deep time.[72] Several paragraphs further, the metaphorically evoked temporal scale of evolution becomes explicit:

> A sense of time lies thick and heavy on such a place. Yearly since the ice age it has awakened each spring to the clangor of cranes . . . An endless caravan of generations has built of its own bones this bridge into the future, this habitat where the oncoming host again may live and breed and die.[73]

For many of Leopold's contemporaries, as for many of our own, another unwelcome implication of the theory of evolution is its purposelessness. In Aristotelian terms, there is no 'final cause' in evolutionary processes, no *telos*, no goal. Evolution proceeds by what the Greeks called chance and necessity—chance genetic mutation, natural selection and a little good or bad luck is what drives evolutionary development. Skunks, mice, hawks, geese, cranes and humans have all just been spit out by the blind forces of nature, from an evolutionary point of view, happy (or unhappy, as the case may be) accidents. For Woody Allen this cosmic purposelessness leads to a profound (and comic) existential funk. If he is at all representative, people seem to want to feel that they have an important place in the grand scheme of things, that their lives have meaning, that we are here for a reason. The Abrahamic (biblical) worldview provides us with an exalted place in the cosmos, tells us the reason why we exist, and gives meaning to our lives; the Darwinian (evolutionary-ecological worldview) does not.

Leopold squarely confronts that obstacle to the popular embrace of the evolutionary-ecological worldview by asking 'To what end?' (this age-old annual cycle of living, breeding and dying). And answers, cryptically, 'Out on the bog a crane, gulping some luckless frog, springs his ungainly bulk into the air and flails the morning sun with mighty wings. The tamaracks re-echo his bugled certitude. He seems to know.'[74]

So deep runs the desire for a transcendent cosmic purpose to give meaning to life that Peter Fritzell, one of the (otherwise probative) contributors to *Companion to A Sand County Almanac*, insisted that Leopold meant that there *is* a final cause, an end, a *telos*—*we* just do not know what it is. But cranes do. Fritzell writes:

> humans do not know, perhaps cannot know, 'to what end', however much they may wish to. The crane, on the other hand, . . . 'seems to know'—not only where

> he came from but also where he and his marshes are
> going—a quality of knowledge man can perceive per-
> haps, but which he cannot capture in language.[75]

I think that Fritzell badly misses Leopold's point. There is no ultimate end. Leopold's point is that the question—To what end?—
does not occur to the crane nor is he troubled by the fact that there
is none. Every day, I read some lines by Matthew Arnold that are
literally inscribed on stone in my study: 'Is it so small a thing /
To have enjoyed the sun, / To have lived light in the spring, / To
have loved, to have thought, to have done?'[76] Why must we have
a preordained *telos* to give meaning to our existence and a *raison d'être*? Isn't that we exist at all enough? Shouldn't we simply
accept the mystery of our existence and pay it the homage that it
deserves by giving it a meaning of our own making?

Wait a while. Perhaps there is an end: an end of another kind
than that desired by those who *do* ask the question and *are* troubled by the absence of a satisfactory scientific answer. Aristotle
draws a distinction that is often forgotten in contemporary tel-
eology/ateleology debates, the distinction between 'extrinsic' or
'transcendent' and 'intrinsic' or 'immanent' ends. Some activities
are their own ends (such as gazing at the moon, playing tennis,
or making love); other activities we do for some end other than
themselves (such as doing onerous, mind-numbing labour for the
sake of earning a wage or travelling a long time in a cramped air-
plane seat to reach a distant destination). For Aristotle, intrinsic
or immanent ends are superior to extrinsic or transcendent ends.
Life might be understood to be an intrinsic or immanent end; we
might live it for its own sake. The crane lives his to its fullest
and with robustness of spirit. That's what the crane knows, if he
knows anything—not where he came from and where he and his
marshes are going. And that's what he has to teach Woody Allen,
Peter Fritzell and any of Leopold's readers who may be alienated
by the *extrinsic, transcendent* purposelessness—the holy *sun-*

yata, the emptiness—at the core of the evolutionary-ecological worldview.

'Marshland Elegy' has a personal significance for me. Not only did it awaken in me the profound potential in the evolutionary-ecological worldview for a naturalistic aesthetic and spirituality, it awakened in me a life-long romance with cranes. '[O]ur appreciation of the crane grows,' Leopold writes,

> with the slow unraveling of earthly history. His tribe, we now know, stems out of the remote Eocene. When we hear his call we hear no mere bird. We hear the trumpet in the orchestra of evolution.[77] He is the symbol of our untamable past, of that incredible sweep of millennia that underlies and conditions the daily affairs of birds and men. And so they live and have their being—these cranes—not in the constricted present, but in the wider reaches of evolutionary time.[78]

After reading this passage for the first time, my very perceptual experience of cranes changed. No longer were they just large birds differing from herons in flying with neck outstretched rather than crooked into an S shape. They were flying fossils, only an evolutionary step or two removed from the pterosaurs from which they evolved. They were to me indeed 'wildness incarnate', a living bridge across the Cretaceous–Tertiary boundary.

In Part II's 'On a Monument to the Pigeon', Leopold meditates at the gravesite of the extinct passenger pigeon in Wyalusing State Park, Wisconsin. In that essay, he further develops the profound potential in the evolutionary-ecological worldview for a naturalistic spirituality and environmental ethic:

> It is a century now since Darwin gave us the first glimpse of the origin of species. We know now what was unknown to all the preceding caravan of generations: that men are only fellow-voyagers with other creatures in the odyssey of evolution. This new knowledge should have given us, by this time, a sense of kinship with fellow creatures; a wish to live and let live; a

sense of wonder over the magnitude and duration of the
biotic enterprise.[79]

Leopold follows with a pot shot at the smug anthropocentrism of
the worldview he essays to remediate:

> Above all we should, in the century since Darwin,
> have come to know that man while now captain of the
> adventuring ship is hardly the sole object of its quest,
> and that his prior assumptions to this effect arose from
> the simple necessity of whistling in the dark.[80]

The argument of Part II: the ecological aspect

The ecological aspect of the evolutionary-ecological worldview
is developed in Part II's 'Odyssey', the essay following, at one
remove, the evolution-themed 'Marshland Elegy'. Prior to European settlement, X, an atom of unspecified species (probably
calcium), is dislodged from the limestone (calcium carbonate)
substrate of the western Wisconsin prairie by a bur oak root. He
begins to cycle through the biota—first into one of the bur oak's
acorns, which is eaten by a deer, which is eaten by an Indian.
After the death and decay of the Indian, it is taken up by bluestem
(a prairie grass) and then goes back into the soil. 'Next he entered
a tuft of side-oats gramma [another prairie grass], a buffalo, a buffalo chip, and again the soil. Next a spiderwort [a prairie flower],
a rabbit, and an owl.' And so the story goes, cycle after cycle,
each one as detailed as the one before. (As an environmental-
education exercise, I observed children set to the task of drawing
and painting X's odyssey. They were kept quiet and busy for a
whole day.) After European settlement, 'Y began a succession of
dizzy annual trips through a new grass called wheat . . . his trip
from rock to river completed in one short century'; and then, in a
flash, from river to 'his ancient prison, the sea'.[81]

At the Yale School of Forestry and Environmental Studies, during the centennial celebration of Leopold's graduation in 2009, the distinguished ecologist Gene Likens, a founder of the famous Hubbard Brook Research Foundation, said that he had spent his whole career just putting numbers on X and Y. And, indeed, when it was first published in 1942, Leopold was expressing, in a scientifically informed literary genre, state-of-the-art ecosystem ecology. In 1935, Arthur Tansley coined the term 'ecosystem'.[82] Tansley expanded the purview of ecology from the biota (relationships among plants and animals) to the 'inorganic "factors" '—for 'there is constant interchange of the most various kinds within each [eco]system, not only between the organisms but between the organic and the inorganic'.[83] Less than a decade after the introduction of the ecosystem idea, Leopold was conceptually, albeit not mathematically, articulating both its main research components—materials cycling, in 'Odyssey' and energy flows in 'A Biotic View of Land'.

Leopold cut, edited and pasted extensive passages from 'A Biotic View of Land', published in 1939, into 'The Land Ethic':

> Plants absorb energy from the sun. This energy flows through a circuit called the biota, which may be represented by a pyramid consisting of layers. The bottom layer is the soil. A plant layer rests on the soil, an insect layer on the plants, a bird and rodent layer on the insects, and so on up through various groups to the apex layer, which consists of the larger carnivores.[84]

A hugely influential historian of ecology, Donald Worster, attributes the energy flow as well as the materials cycling aspects of the eventual ecosystem paradigm in ecology to Tansley, but the word 'energy' does not even occur in the 1935 essay in which Tansley coined the term 'ecosystem'.[85] Raymond Lindeman is properly credited with introducing the energy flow aspect of ecosystem ecology in a 1942 paper, 'The Trophic-Dynamic Aspect of Ecology'.[86] Leopold had articulated the *idea* three years earlier, but has not yet shared the credit with Lindeman. Leopold did not, however, get it quite right—so he may not deserve full credit. Leopold seems to have thought that energy, like materials, cycled:

> Food chains are the living channels which conduct energy upward; death and decay *return it to the soil*. The circuit is not closed; some energy is dissipated in decay, some is added by absorption from the air, some is stored in soils, peats, and long-lived forests; but *it is a sustained circuit*, like a slowly augmented revolving fund of life.[87]

Unlike materials, such as the atoms of 'Odyssey', energy makes a one-way trip through the biota, from solar source to entropic sink.

In the 'Chihuahua and Sonora' section of Part II, Leopold elaborates the 'harmony-of-nature' ecological trope as a two-tiered metaphor. A fast-running mountain stream in northern Mexico, the Gavilan produces an array of sounds, for which there are few adequate words in English. Even Leopold, among the great masters of the language, comes up only with 'the tinkle of waters'.[88] Gently moving waters also gurgle; and rapids roar. Be all that as it may, to characterise the panoply of sounds made by a mountain stream as a 'song' is the first tier of the metaphor; and 'This song of the waters is audible to every ear.'[89] '[B]ut there is other music in these hills, by no means audible to all.' That other 'music' is the second tier of the metaphor.

> To hear even a few notes of it ... you must know the speech of hills and rivers. Then on a still night, when the campfire is low and the Pleiades have climbed over rimrocks, sit quietly and listen for a wolf to howl, and *think hard* of everything you have seen and tried to understand. Then you may hear it—a vast pulsing harmony—its score inscribed on a thousand hills, its notes the lives and deaths of plants and animals, its rhythms spanning the seconds and the centuries.[90]

This 'music' is as cerebral and metaphysical as the Pythagorean harmony of the spheres.

'Thinking Like a Mountain' is all about predator–prey dynamics and the relationship of those dynamics to vegetation cover and soil conservation. In his early Forest Service days, Leopold was a zealous advocate of predator extermination because, as he simply and candidly explains, he 'thought that because fewer wolves meant more deer, that no wolves would mean hunter's paradise'.[91] And so, when given 'a chance to kill a wolf', he and his crew 'were pumping lead into the pack' that had appeared unexpectedly below their encampment on an escarpment—and they succeeded in mortally wounding the alpha female.[92] In perhaps the most oft-quoted lines in Part II, Leopold sounds her death knell:

> We reached the old wolf in time to watch a fierce green fire dying in her eyes. I realized then, and have known ever since, that there was something new to me in those eyes—something known only to her and to the mountain.[93]

Subsequent experience revealed just what the wolf and the mountain knew:

> Since then I have lived to see state after state extirpate its wolves. I have watched the face of many a newly wolfless mountain, and seen the south-facing slopes wrinkle with a maze of new deer trails. I have seen every edible bush and seedling browsed, first to anaemic desuetude, and then to death. I have seen every edible tree defoliated to the height of a saddlehorn . . . In the end the starved bones of the hoped-for deer herd, dead of its own too-much, bleach with the bones of the dead sage, or molder under the high-lined junipers.[94]

The argument of Part III: the axiological and normative implications of an evolutionary-ecological worldview

In addition to the ecological homily about predator–prey dynamics, 'Thinking Like a Mountain' is also, perhaps much more importantly, about a moment of epiphany in the course of Leopold's own process of worldview remediation. Though set in the Southwest and describing an event that took place in 1909, it was written much later, in 1944, in response to criticism by one of Leopold's former students, Albert Hochbaum, who was reading Leopold's manuscript as it was taking shape.[95] In a letter to Leopold he wrote:

> You have sometimes followed trails like anyone else that lead up wrong alleys ... Your lesson is much stronger, then, if you try to show how your own attitude towards your environment has changed ... That's why I suggested the wolf business. I hope that you will have at least one piece on wolves alone.[96]

After reading Leopold's draft of 'Thinking Like a Mountain', Hochbaum replied that it 'fills the bill perfectly'.[97]

In the tale Leopold tells, the dying eyes of the old she-wolf mutely ask her slayer—just as the voice of Jesus asked Saul of Tarsus on the road to Damascus—'Why persecutest thou me?'[98] We too can live and learn, just as did Leopold himself. We too can change our worldview, just as he did. Saul of Tarsus became Paul the Apostle. Aldo Leopold, the zealous predator exterminator—yes, in his Southwest days he was a very zealous advocate of predator extermination—became one of the 20th century's most eloquent advocates and ardent protectors of predators. Both transformations—Saul's and Aldo's—required a profound paradigm shift, a worldview change. Maybe, Leopold hoped, he was but a harbinger of the worldview transformation that society as a whole was poised to undergo. *A Sand County Almanac* is crafted to nudge that process along. The confessional 'Thinking Like a Mountain' demonstrates that worldview remediation is possible. It also demonstrates how a worldview remediator like Leopold can draw on the imagery and power of the very same traditional worldview that he is hoping to replace with the scientific worldview that he is striving to explicate and promulgate.

The penultimate goal of Leopold's central task of worldview remediation is to cultivate in his readers his own settled perception of the world organised by way of the conceptual framework of the seasoned naturalist and professional ecologist that he had become—organised by way of the evolutionary-ecological worldview. In 'Song of the Gavilan' the mode of perception is aural and the goal is to 'hear' the harmony of nature—less with the bodily ear than the ear of the ecologist's mind. In 'Conservation Esthetic' in *Sand County*'s Part III, 'The Upshot', Leopold articulates a visual metaphor complementing the aural metaphor of 'Song of the Gavilan'. The goal is for the reader to come to 'see' the world, if not with the Buddha eye of the classical Japanese Zen master, Dogen, then with the ecological eye of Aldo Leopold—to see with the eye of the ecologist's mind. As Leopold notes in 'Conservation Esthetic', there was no greater American woodsman than Daniel Boone, but

> Boone's reaction depended not only on the quality of what he saw, but on the quality of the *mental eye* with which he saw it. Ecological science has wrought a change in the mental eye. It has disclosed origins and functions for what to Boone were only facts. It has disclosed mechanisms for what to Boone were only attributes . . . [C]ompared with the competent ecologist of the present day, Boone saw only the surface of things. The incredible intricacies of the plant and animal community—the *intrinsic beauty* of the organism called America, then in full bloom of her maidenhood—were as invisible and incomprehensible to Daniel Boone as they are today to Babbitt.[99]

Leopold's ultimate goal is to draw out the axiological and normative implications of the evolutionary-ecological worldview—to bring to light its values and derive from it an environmental ethic. That is the principal burden of Part III of *A Sand County Almanac*, 'The Upshot'.

Here we encounter one of the most disastrous shibboleths of 20th-century philosophy, the so-called 'naturalistic fallacy': the dogma that science and ethics belong to separate universes of discourse, nor ever the twain should have permissible intercourse and legitimate issue. Facts and values, ethics and science, *ises* and *oughts* belong to hermetically sealed compartments of thought and speech.[100] Thus, the very idea that the evolutionary-ecological worldview has ethical and aesthetic implications became a philosophical anathema. The derivation of *oughts* from *ises*, values from facts, ethics from science is alleged to be a fallacy of formal logic.[101] In the 1933 'The Conservation Ethic'—from which Leopold borrowed heavily in composing 'The Land Ethic'—he notes that:

> Some scientists may dismiss this matter [of an evolutionary-ecological conservation ethic] forthwith, on the ground that ecology has no relation to right and wrong. To such I reply that science, *if not philosophy*, should by now have made us cautious about dismissals.[102]

The sciences and the facts they disclose do inform our values and transform our ethics—and well they should. The scientific fact that *Homo sapiens* is a single species, originating in Africa and, from there, spreading all across the planet, makes belief in the superiority of any single human 'race' untenable. Indeed racism is based on the false belief that race is a biological taxon analogous to species, but we know now—thanks to the human genome project, thanks to science—that it is not. We properly correct false values—racism, misogyny, homophobia, xenophobia—by appeal to the facts disclosed by science all the time. And there is nothing in the least fallacious about that.

The axiological implications of the evolutionary-ecological worldview that Leopold derives in 'The Land Ethic' are straightforward and direct.

We might think of anthropocentrism as the view that humans alone have intrinsic value, for whatever reason—in the Abrahamic worldview because humans alone are created in the image of God; in the modern philosophical tradition, best articulated by Immanuel Kant, because humans alone are rational and autonomous. All that is non-human has but instrumental value to intrinsically valuable humans. But the theory of evolution undercuts all the traditional markers of human exceptionalism, as Darwin persuasively demonstrates in *The Descent of Man*.

In accordance with the non-anthropocentrism of the evolutionary-ecological worldview that Leopold is exposing and promulgating in *A Sand County Almanac*, he effectively attributes intrinsic value to 'land'. Anything that has mere instrumental value can, as Kant himself noted, be assigned a price, by means of which its relative instrumental value can be expressed:

> Whatever has reference to general human inclinations [human desires or preferences] and needs has a market price; whatever, without supposing any need, accords with a certain taste [objects of aesthetic delight, such as environmental 'amenities'] . . . has an effective price [a shadow price]; but that which constitutes the condition under which alone something can be an end in itself has not merely a relative worth, i.e., a price, but has an intrinsic worth, i.e., a dignity.[103]

While Leopold does not specifically say that land has 'intrinsic value', he uses words that clearly indicate that that is what he has in mind. Moreover, like Kant, he contrasts things that have intrinsic value with those that have merely instrumental value by associating the latter with economic valuation. Here is what Leopold does say about the value of land:

> It is inconceivable to me that an ethical relation to land
> can exist without love, respect, and a high regard for its
> value. By value, I of course mean something far broader
> than mere economic value: I mean value in the philo-
> sophical sense.[104]

In contrasting the kind of value that he is thinking of with 'mere
economic value'—price, to which everything of instrumental
value is subject—by 'value in the philosophical sense', Leopold
could only mean what we environmental philosophers call intrinsic value.

The normative implications of the evolutionary-ecological
worldview that Leopold derives in 'The Land Ethic' are also
straightforward and direct, but a little more complex.

From Darwin himself in *The Descent of Man*, Leopold took the
idea that human ethics evolved by natural selection as a means to
social integration. As Darwin colourfully put it, 'No tribe could
hold together if murder, robbery, treachery, &c., were common;
consequently such crimes within the limits of the same tribe "are
branded with everlasting infamy"; but excite no such sentiments
beyond these limits.'[105] If a tribe could not hold together, then, as
solitaries, its erstwhile members could hardly survive and repro-
duce. Their murderous, larcenous and treacherous genes would
be winnowed from the gene pool, while those of the compassion-
ate, sympathetic and sociable members of well-integrated coop-
erative communities would be conserved. As Leopold puts into a
nutshell Darwin's evolutionary account of the origin of ethics:

> All ethics so far *evolved* rest upon a single premise: that
> the individual is a member of a community of interde-
> pendent parts. His instincts prompt him to compete for
> his place in that community, but his ethics prompt him
> also to co-operate (perhaps in order that there may be a
> place to compete for).[106]

Darwin then imagined how 'these limits'—the tribal boundaries—
might have been expanded and with them human ethics:

> As man advances in civilization, and small tribes are united into larger communities, the simplest reason would tell each individual that he ought to extend his social instincts and sympathies to all the members of the same nation, though personally unknown to him. This point being once reached, there is only an artificial barrier to prevent his sympathies extending to the men of all nations and races.[107]

During the same year that Leopold put the finishing touches on his masterpiece (also the year of his death), 1948, the United Nations issued its Universal Declaration of Human Rights, fulfilling—at least in principle—Darwin's vision of mankind's social instincts and sympathies extending to the men (and women) of all nations and races. But Leopold's vision went further still. To the evolutionary foundations provided by Darwin, Leopold added those of ecology: ecology 'simply enlarges the boundary of the community to include soils, waters, plants, and animals, or collectively the land'.[108] And an evolutionary-ecological land ethic, according to Leopold, 'changes the role of *Homo sapiens* from conqueror of the land-community to plain member and citizen of it. It implies respect for his fellow-members and also respect for the community as such'.[109] From these evolutionary and ecological conceptual foundations, Leopold famously distilled a summary moral maxim, a golden rule: 'A thing is right when it tends to preserve the integrity, stability, and beauty of the biotic community. It is wrong when it tends otherwise.'[110]

The writing

Leopold's project in *A Sand County Almanac*—the exposition and promulgation of an evolutionary-ecological worldview and its axiological and normative implications—is a grand one, to be sure. He is trying to effect a sea change in popular consciousness.

The actual evolutionary and ecological concepts that he exposes and promulgates are, however, pretty basic. Necessarily so, given the lay audience he is addressing and its limited capacity for either profundity or subtlety. Indeed, Leopold produced exactly the book that Knopf first said they wanted him to write: 'a personal book recounting adventures in the field . . . warmly, evocatively, and vividly written . . . a book for the layman . . . [with] room for the author's opinions on ecology and conservation . . . worked into a framework of actual field experience'. That sort of book does not lend itself to a sustained, well-developed discussion of evolutionary biology and ecology, let alone value theory and moral philosophy. Why then has it become a great book? It is, by no means, unique, the only book of its kind from its era. There is, for example, *Road to Survival* by William Vogt, published in 1948 by the same publisher that was favourably considering Leopold's manuscript but that did not do so as quickly as OUP.[111] Even more similar to *A Sand County Almanac* is *Adventures with a Texas Naturalist* by Roy Bedichek, published in 1947, two years *before* Leopold's book appeared—so there can be no suspicion that Bedichek was imitating or echoing Leopold. In his introduction to a recent new edition, contemporary nature writer Rick Bass writes, perceptively, that Bedichek's *Adventures with a Texas Naturalist* 'has much the same strength and message as Leopold's *A Sand County Almanac*'.[112] If so, why have few outside a small circle of Texan environmentalists and historians ever heard of Roy Bedichek or his book? And the flipside of that question: why the virtual canonisation of Leopold and the veneration of *Sand County*?

The simple and shallow answer is that Leopold had the good sense to write a slender volume of short essays—the longest of which, 'The Land Ethic', is just 25 pages—in all, just 226 pages, typeset in a large font size and illustrated by some 30 or so drawings (by Charles W. Schwartz), about half of which occupy a full page. Bedichek's book is half again as many pages long with half again as many words to a page and with half the number of illustrations (by Ward Lockwood). Leopold knew how to give his message impact. His prose is condensed, heavy with import. It makes its mark in the mind and leaves a lasting impression. His book has risen above others like it from the same era mainly because of the way in which it is written.

John Tallmadge's 'Anatomy of a Classic' in *Companion to A Sand County Almanac* provides an analysis of Leopold's style. Central to it are Leopold's use of 'techniques of compression'.[113] One such technique is 'concentration'. While recording many natural facts, only those that 'serve the theme and thrust of the essay' are included—'eliminating whatever does not advance the plot'.[114] As a result, 'Each word drops into place with that sense of inevitability that Dylan Thomas said he found in all good poetry ... as if chosen with the utmost care.'[115] Another technique is 'engagement'—inviting 'the reader to contribute [what] the text does not provide, thereby reducing the amount of explanation while increasing the density of implication'.[116] Leopold's devices of engagement are 'synecdoche, allusion, irony, understatement, and rhetorical questions'.[117] I have already noted and commented on Leopold's use of synecdoche. In addition to 'Abraham' as a surrogate for the Bible, Leopold frequently makes 'Babbitt' a surrogate for the typical mindless American cipher. In other passages already quoted we find examples of all these devices. As Tallmadge notes,

> Because the narrator does not browbeat us with verbiage, we feel respected, as if he valued our time, and so we are more inclined to listen. Here we feel is a writer who has taken pains to find exactly the right words to express the distilled wisdom of his life.[118]

One important aspect of Leopold's style, noted by Tallmadge, is its biblical resonance, especially resonance with the parables of Jesus in the New Testament:

> A parable conveys novel ideas by means of famil-
> iar facts and situations, as in the well-known para-
> bles of Jesus ... Eventually we realize that Leopold's
> 'sketches' are really parables and that this parabolic
> style accounts more than anything else for the book's
> perennial freshness.[119]

As I have noted here, in addition to parables, 'Thinking Like a Mountain' almost transparently mirrors the dramatic the story of Paul's conversion on the Road to Damascus.

In the 1920s Leopold gave close study to the Bible—not, I think, for devotional as much as for rhetorical inspiration.[120] During this time he wrote a playful, irreverent piece titled 'The Forestry of the Prophets', based on 'a purely amateur study of the Books of the Prophets of the Old Testament' from which he gleaned and commented on the occasional bits of forest lore that they contain.[121] In other essays from the same period, one finds Leopold making obvious attempts to mimic biblical diction and phrasing. For example, in a posthumously published typescript, 'Some Fundamentals of Conservation in the Southwest', dated 1923, Leopold writes, 'Erosion eats into our hills like a conta-gion, and floods bring down the loosened soil upon our valleys like a scourge.'[122] By the time he assembled his masterpiece, he had perfected his rhetorical skills; but as Tallmadge notes, 'Like hand-rubbed wood, its surface conceals its craft.'[123] So, for exam-ple, in a passage already quoted from 'Marshland Elegy' Leopold employs a biblical phrase, but redacts it just enough that its effect on the reader is more subliminal than conscious: 'And so they live and have their being—these cranes . . .' Had he written—as he may have at first been tempted to—'And so they live, *and move*, and have their being—these cranes', the full phrase would be immediately recognisable as biblical.[124] And thus its sublimi-nal effect and power would have been cancelled.

The ultimate use of irony, then, in *A Sand County Almanac*, is Leopold's deployment of the rhetorical power of biblical phrasing (e.g. 'live and have their being'), biblical narratives (e.g. Paul on the road to Damascus) and biblical literary forms (e.g. parables) to undercut the Bible-based aspect of the worldview that he sought to replace with the evolutionary-ecological worldview. To undercut its other aspects—consumerism and the associated commodification of nature and the reduction of its value to dollars and cents and the reduction of its wholeness to an aggregate of parts—Leopold deploys all these Bible-derived rhetorical devices, such as the frequent use of the 'Babbitt' synecdoche, and the many more in his rhetorical arsenal that Tallmadge identifies, irony principal among them. We have been conditioned to hear the words of the Bible as revealed truth. Thanks to Leopold's well-concealed craft, we receive the words of *A Sand County Almanac* as similarly revealed truth. It is no wonder, nor is it any accident, that Leopold is called a prophet and his wonderful book is called a Bible.[125]

The new shifting paradigm in ecology and the evolutionary-ecological worldview

A Sand County Almanac was published more than half a century ago and, between then and now, both evolutionary biology and certainly ecology have undergone a series of profound changes. Is the evolutionary-ecological worldview that *Sand County* so persuasively exposes and promulgates still tenable? Does the Leopold land ethic, grounded in that worldview, remain relevant to our present environmental concerns?

The land ethic obviously seems to assume as definitive the biotic-community paradigm most clearly and elegantly expressed by the aforementioned Charles Elton in *Animal Ecology*, in which he represents plants and animals as occupying 'niches', playing 'roles' and pursuing 'professions' in the 'economy of nature'.[126]

After the deconstruction of the 'community unit' theory by the likes of R.H. Whittaker, John T. Curtis and Robert P. McIntosh, do ecologists still believe that biotic communities exist as robust entities?[127] And, if they do, do biotic communities have any integrity and stability to be preserved?

Philosophers call questions about the existence of this or that *ontological* questions. Does God exist? Do Platonic forms exist? Do ghosts exist? Do electrons exist? Do quarks exist? Do biotic communities exist? Existence may come in degrees. As the aforementioned Tansley noted in the paper in which he coined the word *ecosystem*,

> the systems we isolate mentally are not only included as parts of larger ones, but they also overlap, interlock, and interact with one another. The *isolation is partly artificial*, but it is the only possible way in which we can proceed.[128]

Do ecosystems exist?—say, the Greater Yellowstone ecosystem or a prairie soil ecosystem? Yes, but when we come to isolate them, to bound them, for purposes of ecological study, we partly create them. Perhaps we might best say that ecosystems exist potentially, like electrons, and their existence is fully actualised when ecologists isolate them for purposes of study, just as electrons emerge fully into existence when quantum physicists measure them.

Leopold's project of worldview remediation in *A Sand County Almanac* is far more artful and beguiling than it had been a decade earlier. In a piece titled 'The Arboretum and the University', published in 1934, Leopold more harshly perp-walked the prevailing cultural 'world view' (his term) and boldly looked to ecology for a replacement:

> For twenty centuries or longer, all civilized *thought* has rested on one basic premise: that it is the destiny of man to exploit and enslave the earth. The biblical injunction to 'go forth and multiply' is merely one of many dogmas which imply this attitude of *philosophical* imperialism.

> During the past few decades, however, a new science
> called ecology has been unobtrusively spreading a film
> of doubt over this heretofore unchallenged 'world view'.
> Ecology tells us that no animal—not even man—can be
> regarded as independent of his environment. Plants,
> animals, men, and soil are a community of interde-
> pendent parts, *an organism*. No organism can survive
> the decadence of a member. Mr. Babbitt is no more a
> separate entity than is his left arm or a single cell of his
> biceps . . . It may flatter our ego to be called the sons of
> man, but it would be nearer the truth to call ourselves
> the brothers of our fields and forests.[129]

The (evolutionary-) ecological worldview Leopold here alludes
to is the superorganism paradigm championed by F.E. Clements,
the dean of American ecology during its first quarter-century
of existence as a distinct scientific discipline.[130] The next year
(1935), Tansley introduced a new paradigm in ecology—the ecosystem paradigm—which is often characterised as a radical depar-
ture from Clementsian organicism.[131] While denying that 'mature,
well-integrated plant communities' were well enough integrated
to qualify as organisms, Tansley repeatedly declares that they are
'quasi-organisms', existing in a state of 'dynamic equilibrium',
evolved to persist in that happy state by 'natural selection'.[132] By
mid-century, E.P. Odum had virtually returned the dominant ecosystem paradigm in ecology to its Clementsian roots, characteris-
ing ecosystems in organismic terms.[133] *A Sand County Almanac*
reflects the state of ambiguity in ecology about the (evolution-
ary-) ecological worldview at mid-century. As noted, the dominant image of land that Leopold promulgates there is the Eltonian
'biotic community'. But, with his 'fountain-of-energy' trope, first
published a decade before he edited and pasted it into 'The Land
Ethic', Leopold also anticipated the way that Raymond Lindeman
would integrate Tansley's ecosystem concept with Elton's pyra-
mid of numbers and render Elton's qualitative idea of food chains
quantitatively as 'conduits of measurable energy'.[134] Leopold also

invoked the idea of 'land health'.[135] But health is a state of an organism; and, indeed, in the same passage, Leopold used the phrase 'land the collective *organism*'.[136] On the other hand, he expressed reservations about the 'balance-of-nature' idea and invoked 'the mental image of land as a biotic *mechanism*'.[137] So, is land an organism, a biotic community, an energy-flow and nutrient-cycling ecosystem, or is it a mechanism?

Late-20th-century hierarchy theory actually provides a theoretical integration of these once disparate paradigms in ecology.[138] Community ecology focuses on interactive *components*, the specific plants and animals that perform various jobs in the economy of nature. Ecosystem ecology focuses on the *processes* that those components carry out, irrespective of the specific identity of the components; and it focuses on fluxes of energy and materials through the system. In hierarchy theory, three hierarchical levels must be isolated: the mid-level may be regarded as the 'organic' object of inquiry; the level beneath it consists of various 'mechanisms' and the level above it is the 'context' or 'environment' on which it draws for materials and energy.[139] Consider oneself as an organic object of study. One's various organs—the heart pumping blood, the lungs oxygenating the blood, the kidneys cleansing the blood—are the mechanisms that, when appropriately integrated and coordinated, perform organic functions. And one's environment is the context in which one exists and the source of one's energy and materials in the form of food (other organisms), air and water. Analogously, consider Lindeman's Cedar Bog Lake as the organic object of his ecological study. The photosynthesis of the algae and other aquatic plants and the dynamics of the food web and its predator–prey interactions are the mechanisms, and the surrounding watershed is the context or environment. Arguably, in mixing his ecological metaphors in the way that he does in *Sand County*, Leopold vaguely anticipates the development of hierarchy theory in ecology.

In the decades following the publication of *Sand County*, the truly radical contemporary critique of Clementsian organicism by H.A. Gleason—which made Tansley's seem tame by comparison—was revived as the 'individualistic paradigm' in ecology, according to which each species is 'law unto itself' and biotic communities are coincidental aggregates of species adapted to similar environmental gradients.[140] The ecological impact of natural disturbance was acknowledged and emphasised and 'disturbance regimes' were identified.[141] Anthropogenic disturbance, moreover, was recognised to be long-standing and ubiquitous, requiring humans to be factored in to ecological studies on a par with other ecologically significant agents.[142] Urban ecology thus emerged as no less worthy or oxymoronic a field of study in ecology than tropical ecology or grassland ecology.[143]

So, from our vantage point in the second decade of the 21st century, we might well ask, Is there anything that can be characterised as an evolutionary-*ecological* worldview? (Since the 1930s, at the conceptual grain of a worldview, evolutionary theory has changed only around the margins and in the details, while ecological theory has been far more volatile.) And, if so, in what does an evolutionary-*ecological* worldview consist? Does ecology, that is, no less than the theory of evolution, provide us with a network of concepts, a cognitive framework, that functions as a lens through which our sensory experience is classified and organised to form a coherent whole, an evolutionary *cum* ecological worldview? I believe that it does, but it poses as formidable an expository challenge to contemporary philosophers as it did to Leopold. His challenge was that of a trailblazer into *terra incognita*; Leopold pioneered the philosophy of ecology. Our challenge is to follow him, but we must do so into a denser and more tangled thicket of scientific ideas than those that he encountered. For all the competing metaphors that ecology had spawned by the mid-20th century—superorganism, biotic community/economy of nature, ecosystem, mechanism—few doubted that biotic communities were ontologically robust and had integrities and were stable. Now ecologists present us with a view of a world that is dynamic at every scale, with no stable equilibrium in sight, a world constantly undergoing disturbance, dissolution and reorganisation. A land ethic without reference to integrity and stability is possible, as I have argued elsewhere.[144] It is just not as easy as it was a half-century or so ago to articulate a coherent evolutionary-ecological worldview and work through its axiological and normative implications.

However formidable the task before us, humanists of the third millennium must rise to the challenge. The future of global civilisation is at grave risk of collapse if the prevailing collective delusion—the old 'Abrahamic view of land' married to cornucopian consumerism—is allowed to stand unopposed and unreplaced. Like Leopold before us, we have to call it out by name and not shrink from enumerating its many absurdities and megalomaniacal conceits. But that is only half the task. Like Leopold before us, we also have viscerally to appreciate and effectively to communicate the very real aesthetic and spiritual potentiality of the evolutionary-ecological worldview that we have to offer as an alternative—thanks in large part to him. The Abrahamic worldview has a legion of critics—from the Lynn Whites and Ian McHargs of the 1960s to the Richard Dawkinses and Bill Mahers of the present.[145] Leopold may not be alone in appreciating the positive aesthetic and spiritual potentiality in the scientific worldview—Thomas Berry also comes to mind—but he is one of the few who did.[146] So let us seize the standard from the prematurely fallen Leopold and press forward with the creative and affirmative as well as the critical vocation to which he was called.[147]

3

Rachel Carson's *Silent Spring*
A legacy for sustainable development

José Lima Santos

Rachel Carson's book on the impacts of pesticide use on humanity and nature—*Silent Spring*—changed the way we perceive our relationships with nature, particularly those mediated through science and technology. The aim of this chapter is to discuss Carson's book, not only as regards its success in changing the hearts and minds of her fellow citizens, but also as an important legacy for a deeper understanding of the many challenges we still face today in building a more sustainable future.

The author and her personal and cultural context are introduced first, as well as the historical context of the book. The communication strategy and personal skills used by the author in writing *Silent Spring* are discussed as key factors in determining the book's impact on the emerging environmental movement of the 1960s and early 1970s, which led to the creation of today's environmental policy.

Based on selected excerpts from the book, we identify some elements of the environmental agenda that Rachel Carson promoted with her book: (1) the role of science in helping us work with nature, as opposed to against it; (2) the type of humble science that is required to set us on (what we would today call) a path of sustainable development; (3) the public's right to know about possible health and well-being consequences of environmentally risky decisions, and to participate in these decisions; (4) the role of scientists in communicating science with the public and informing the public debate—a role that Carson played with supreme skill in the field of pesticide use and crop protection, showing the way ahead for many other environmental fields; and (5) the interplay of truth, interest and economic incentives in the daily work of scientists, when creating scientific knowledge, technical solutions and the resulting potential impacts on nature. We also underline the relevance of these issues for a deeper understanding of the major challenges we still face today when promoting sustainable development.

The author

Rachel was born in Springdale, Pennsylvania, in 1907. As a child, she inherited a life-long love of nature and the living world from her mother. According to her biographer Linda Lear, 'Rachel Carson first discovered nature in the company of her mother, a devotee of the nature study movement. She wandered the banks of the Allegheny River . . . , observing the wildlife and plants around her and particularly curious about the habits of birds.'[148]

Rachel's writing ability was evident from an early age: she was only ten years old when she published her first story in a children's literary magazine. She first studied marine biology at the Woods Hole Biological Laboratory, and graduated in zoology from the Johns Hopkins University in 1932. Then, she started writing radio scripts on marine life for the US Bureau of Fisheries, and also published articles about the natural history of the Chesapeake Bay for the *Baltimore Sun*.

From 1936 to 1952, she worked for the US Fish and Wildlife Service (USFWS), where, due to her writing skills, she became editor-in-chief for all its publications.

In 1941, she published the book *Under the Sea-wind: A Naturalist's Picture of Ocean Life*, described by Linda Lear as 'a masterpiece of nature-immersion'.

In 1951, she published the book *The Sea Around Us*, a geographic and oceanographic book written for the general public, and, in 1955, *The Edge of the Sea*, a practical guide for identifying creatures living in marshes, tidal pools and other aquatic habitats on the sea's edge. These two books made Carson

> the foremost science writer in America. She understood that there was a deep need for writers who could report on and interpret the natural world. Readers around the world found comfort in her clear explanations of complex science . . . and her obvious love for the wonders of nature. Hers was a trusted voice in a world riddled by uncertainty.[149]

In 1956, Carson finished writing an article 'Help Your Child to Wonder' for the magazine *Woman's Home Companion*, which was published posthumously as a book, *The Sense of Wonder*. This book is very telling about the author's purposes for writing it: motivating adults to feed the innate awe felt by children in their experiences of the natural world.

In June 1962, she started publishing *Silent Spring*, first in instalments in the *New Yorker*, and eventually as a book in September of the same year. According to Carson, the writing of *Silent Spring* was motivated by a letter she received in 1958 from a friend, Olga Owens Huckins, who was deeply upset about the mass killing of birds that occurred in Cape Cod after DDT was sprayed in the area. In her own words, Olga 'told me of her own bitter experience of a small world made lifeless, and so brought my attention back to a problem with which I had long been concerned. I thus realized I must write this book.'[150]

During 1963, in the follow-up to the publication of *Silent Spring*, Carson testified before Senate committees on matters related to the misuse of pesticides. She died in 1964, aged 56, after a long battle against cancer.

The book's impact

Silent Spring was published after one and a half decades of post-war economic growth, at the height of the Cold War and times of great suspicion and intolerance, when science and technology were seen as America's main allies in defeating its enemies on both the economic and military battlefields. They were also perceived as part of a project in which nature submitted entirely to humanity; in particular, the chemical industry and DDT were the actors and heroes of all these conquests and victories, promising to destroy hordes of pests that threatened human food and health.[151]

As regards farming, all this was set against a background of the post-war expansion of a new, chemically based technological model, which multiplied the world's cereal output threefold with the help of genetically improved plant varieties and industry-based agricultural inputs, such as fertilisers and pesticides; this was done as part of a process of accelerated and global transformation of agro-ecosystems through the substitution of artificial inputs (such as industrial nitrogen fertilisers or pesticides) for natural processes (such as nitrogen fixation by soil bacteria, or insect population control by natural predators). As a result, the way ecosystems functioned was totally transformed on a global level, with nitrogen fertiliser manufacturing acting today as a major means of nitrogen entering ecosystems from the atmosphere—in fact, today, the fertiliser industry represents half of the planetary nitrogen cycle.[152]

Carson's book challenged all of these recent and acclaimed achievements, provoking an intense debate about the use of pesticides and the overall programme of humankind's subjugation of nature, of which pesticides were only a part.

On the other hand, there were some aspects of the cultural and socio-economic context of the book that clearly favoured the emergence of that debate. First, there was an increasing awareness of the environmental impacts of pesticide use. Second, postwar growth had promoted the emergence of a middle class with leisure time, disposable income and their own cars, as well as a clear interest in outdoor recreation and an improved quality of life, which depended on good environmental quality and healthy ecosystems. Third, the first weaknesses and setbacks of humanity's programme to dominate nature through pesticides—such as pest populations developing resistance and the appearance of new plagues—began to occur. Eventually, the growth and sufficiency of agricultural output, and the creation of the first agricultural surpluses, reduced the pressure to increase yields through the use of chemicals.

Carson was quick to read this context and understand who her allies were—belonging to the emerging middle class and being personally involved in outdoor activities and the study of nature probably helped her in this. Based on an extensive research effort, she then wrote the book that launched the debate.

Silent Spring is an excellent piece of argumentation, advocacy and communication, in which the allegations are clearly made from the very beginning, and the facts that are invoked and discussed speak for themselves. Actually, chapters 2 and 17 of the book—the former about the 'right to know', where the main allegations are made, and the latter about 'the other way', where the

final allegations about pesticide use and alternatives are made—
are quite similar in their form to the allegations made by lawyers
in court.

Silent Spring triggered a wave of resentment from the chemical
industry. It was argued that Carson did not consider the benefits
of pesticide use and that by following her advice we would return
to the old days of famine, poverty and illness. One of her critics
went as far as to say that '. . . there has not been a mass murderer
executed in the past half-century who has been responsible for as
many deaths of human beings as the sainted Rachel Carson'.

Farmers and scientists from the US Department of Agriculture
(USDA) argued that without pesticides yields would dramatically decline and agriculture would no longer be able to feed the
world.

However, the outcome of the debate was favourable to Carson
and to her clear and evidence-based arguments. According to
Linda Lear, the chemical industry's attack on Carson was seen
with distrust by the general public, who viewed her as a sincere
woman and reputed writer and scientist. Lear also underlines
the importance of Rachel's use of concrete and well-documented
cases to prove her allegations, the inclusion of public perceptions
(quoting many people's letters and testimonies), the 55 pages of
references (unusual in a book for the general public), the list of
scientists who reviewed the book, and especially Carson's decision to write for the public and not for scientists, experts or deci-
sion-makers, as factors that explain the success and influence of
the book.

Silent Spring clearly raised the awareness about the risks associated with pesticide use, which was quick to trigger citizen
action opposing particular pesticide spreading programmes—e.g.
residents of Squirrel Island, in Maine, rejected in a referendum
an aerial spraying programme already planned for that area.

In the longer term, the book played a significant role in launch-
ing the environmental movement on both sides of the Atlantic

and supporting the idea that we all have a fundamental right to a clean environment, which today is reflected in the modern constitutions of many countries, including Portugal, and the Treaties of the European Union.

The debate launched by *Silent Spring* eventually led legislators to pass new laws and governments to create new agencies for better regulation of pesticide use and environmental pollution in general. The creation of the US Environmental Protection Agency (EPA) in 1970 and the transfer of regulatory powers previously attributed to the USDA to this new agency can be traced back to Carson's concerns and the awareness she helped raise. The period between 1970 and the following two years saw the first celebration of Earth Day, the Paris summit (which created the Directorate-General for the Environment of the European Commission), the Stockholm Conference on the Human Environment and the creation of the United Nations Environment Programme (UNEP).

These were the most visible global results of the growing environmental movement of the 1960s and early 1970s, but much still remained to be done, as shown by the recent conclusion of the programme reviewing registered pesticides in the European Union, which reduced the authorised number of active substances in pesticides from 1,000 to 240 between 1993 and 2007. Many active substances were removed from the market simply because it was impossible to demonstrate that they were safe for human health and the environment. We note here a crucial inversion of the burden of proof: in the past, Carson had to prove the dangers of pesticides to launch the debate; now, the industry has to prove they are safe. The world has come a long way and Carson was one of the pioneers in paving it. A happy coincidence is worth highlighting here: in a leaflet published by the European Commission about sustainable use of pesticides and the removal of the most dangerous pesticides from the market, there is a picture of a (European) robin eating an earthworm. This bird is the

European equivalent of the American robin, which was used by Carson in one of her multiple case studies on how the environment was being poisoned with pesticides and how birds were being killed en masse through eating poisoned earthworms. All this helps us trace many of our current successes in improving environmental conditions back to Rachel Carson's book.

The environmental agenda in *Silent Spring*

In addition to creating the public awareness that would form the basis of the emerging environmental movement and resulting environmental policies and institutions, in *Silent Spring* Carson developed many ideas that are still relevant to the many challenges and dilemmas we face today when attempting to create a more sustainable future. The concept of sustainable development did not exist in the 1960s; however, its logic would most likely have been easily accepted by Carson. On the other hand, many ideas she developed are very relevant to us now and to sustainable development in particular—especially those ideas related to working with nature (and not against it), to the type of science that we need, and to the role science should play, not only in obtaining technological solutions for our problems but also in helping the public to understand the challenges we face, and so promote public debate on issues of environment and technology. In this section, we use extensive excerpts from *Silent Spring* to illustrate these ideas and their potential for us today.

Working with (as opposed to against) nature

The first idea is that of understanding and using the complex and effective processes developed by nature to deal with its own problems (e.g. pest population control by biotic interactions) in our favour, instead of trying to substitute these processes with simpler industrial products (such as pesticides), which are undoubtedly riskier in the short term and less effective in the long term. In addition to this, in the long term, these substitutions create new problems which they cannot solve, such as the development of pesticide resistance by pests or the elimination of pest predators, and thus the destruction of many useful natural processes.

This idea is opposed to the post-war project of replacing natural processes occurring in agro-ecosystems (ecosystem services in today's vocabulary) with technological products, which characterises the chemical-mechanical paradigm in agricultural technology. It creates the basis for a new, ecologically based paradigm for agricultural technology. Today this paradigm is being explored by agro-ecology, eco-agriculture[153] and other research areas that are core to the sustainable development of food production and to food security, in a world with rising population levels, increasing food demands and shrinking water, soil and biodiversity resources. We selected some quotations from *Silent Spring* where this idea of working with nature and its potential are fully and clearly explained in the context of pest control in forests. In Carson's own words:

> The predator and the preyed upon exist not alone, but as part of a vast web of life, all of which needs to be taken into account.
> ... with a minimum of help and a maximum of noninterference from man, Nature can have her way, setting up all that wonderful and intricate system of checks and balances that protects the forest from undue damage by insects.[154]

> Birds, ants, forest spiders, and soil bacteria are as much a part of a forest as the trees, in the view of European foresters, who take care to inoculate a new forest with these protective factors.
> The encouragement of birds is one of the first steps. In the modern era of intensive forestry the old hollow trees are gone and with them homes for woodpeckers

and other tree-nesting birds. This lack is met by nesting boxes, which draw the birds back into the forest.

Other boxes are specially designed for owls and for bats, so that these creatures may take over in the dark hours the work of insect hunting performed in daylight by small birds.[155]

There is a whole battery of armaments available to the forester who is willing to look for permanent solutions that preserve and strengthen the natural relations in the forest.

Chemical pest control in the forest is at best a stop-gap measure bringing no real solution, at worst killing the fish in the forest streams, bringing on plagues of insects, and destroying the natural controls and those we may be trying to introduce.

By such violent measures, ... the partnership for life of the forest is entirely being unbalanced, and the catastrophes caused by parasites repeat in shorter and shorter periods . . .[156]

Through all these new, imaginative, and creative approaches to the problem of sharing our earth with other creatures there runs a constant theme, the awareness that we are dealing with life—with living populations and all their pressures and counter-pressures, their surges and recessions.

Only by taking account of such life forces and by cautiously seeking to guide them into channels favorable to ourselves can we hope to achieve a reasonable accommodation between the insect hordes and ourselves.[157]

A humble science: learning from past failures

Working with nature requires a humble science founded on a modest epistemology, which is explicitly defended by Carson on many occasions in the book, such as these:

The current vogue for poisons has failed utterly to take into account these most fundamental considerations.

As crude a weapon as the cave man's club, the chemical barrage has been hurled against the fabric of life—a fabric on the one hand delicate and destructible, on the other miraculously tough and resilient, and capable of striking back in unexpected ways.

These extraordinary capacities of life have been ignored by the practitioners of chemical control who have brought to their task no 'high-minded orientation,' no humility before the vast forces with which they tamper.[158]

The 'control of nature' is a phrase conceived in arrogance, born of the Neanderthal age of biology and philosophy, when it was supposed that nature exists for the convenience of man.

The concepts and practices of applied entomology for the most part date from that Stone Age of science. It is our alarming misfortune that so primitive a science has armed itself with the most modern and terrible weapons, and that in turning them against the insects it has also turned them against the earth.[159]

At the end of a decade or more of intensive chemical control, entomologists were finding that problems they had considered solved a few years earlier had returned to plague them. And new problems had arisen as insects once present only in insignificant numbers had increased to the status of serious pests.

By their very nature, chemical controls are self-defeating, for they have been devised and applied without taking into account the complex biological systems against which they have been blindly hurled.

The chemicals may have been pretested against a few individual species, but not against living communities.[160]

Here, Carson implicitly admits that real tests of ecological effectiveness can only be carried out in nature, not inside the laboratory. We could only have learned what we have about the effects of pesticide use by experimenting with nature. In this sense, what should be most criticised are the scale we adopted for these 'experiments' and the fact that we have not rigorously monitored their results, both of which reveal that these 'spraying experiments' were not actually intended as experiments but as large-scale applications of supposedly pre-tested and safe technologies. Many of these criticisms could be applied to the way we choose large-scale applications of genetically modified crops or biofuel production targets without such ecological tests regarding safety or effectiveness, raising many concerns about sustainability.

The importance Carson places on the rigorous monitoring of our experiments with nature is stated in many parts of the book:

> All these facts are known because the Fisheries Research Board of Canada had been conducting a salmon study on the Northwest Miramichi since 1950. Each year it had made a census of the fish living in this stream . . . With this complete record of prespraying condition, it was possible to measure the damage done by the spraying with an accuracy that has seldom been matched elsewhere.[161]

Ultimately, we might consider that Carson was mostly interested in criticising the arrogant attitude of modern scientists towards their subject: that is, towards the balance of nature.

> . . . nowadays it is fashionable to dismiss the balance of nature as a state of affairs that prevailed in an earlier, simpler world—a state that has now been so thoroughly upset that we might as well forget it.
>
> Some find this a convenient assumption, but as a chart for a course of action it is highly dangerous. The balance of nature is not the same today that in Pleistocene times, but it is still there: a complex, precise and highly integrated system of relationships between living things which cannot safely be ignored any more than the law of gravity can be defied with impunity by a man perched on the edge of a cliff.
>
> The balance of nature is not a status quo; it is fluid, ever shifting, in a constant state of adjustment. Man, too, is part of this balance. Sometimes the balance is

in his favor; sometimes—and all too often through his
own activities—it is shifted to his disadvantage.[162]

All this recommends a humble, modest epistemology and a
technology that is careful with and respectful towards nature, as
well as serious monitoring of the outcomes of our experiments
with nature to ensure that we can eventually learn from our own
mistakes. So, ultimately, a respectful attitude towards nature
should be created, perhaps through a pedagogy that encourages
the sense of wonder in relation to nature that is innate in children, as recommended by Carson (in *The Sense of Wonder*); or by
developing a new role for science and scientists as informers of
citizens and the public debate (a role that Carson practised more
than preached) and not only as creators of technologically valued
knowledge.

The basis for scientific humbleness is not only related to knowledge creation and limits to it (that is: epistemological) but ontological as well, because we are part of nature—as stated in the
previous excerpt. As such, we suffer because of nature's imbal-
ances in the same way as other companion creatures, an idea
clearly developed by Carson when discussing environmental dis-
ease in humans:

> Where do pesticides fit into the picture of environmen-
> tal disease? We have seen that they now contaminate
> soil, water, and food, that they have the power to make
> our streams fishless and our gardens and woodlands
> silent and birdless. Man, however much he may like to
> pretend the contrary, is part of nature. Can he escape a
> pollution that is now so thoroughly distributed through-
> out our world?
>
> For each of us, as for the robin in Michigan or the
> salmon in the Miramichi, this is a problem of ecology,
> of interrelationships, of interdependence. We poison
> the caddis flies in a stream and the salmon runs dwin-
> dle and die . . . We spray our elms and the following
> springs are silent of robin song, not because we sprayed
> the robins directly but because the poison traveled, step

by step, through the now familiar elm leaf–earthworm–robin cycle.[163]

The right to know and to decide about risky options

In chapter 2 of *Silent Spring* ('Obligation to Endure'), the main allegations of the book are made clear, and some allegations, which could be falsely attributed to her (such as that she was against pesticide use in any circumstances), are explicitly discarded. For Carson, everything in the book is related to our *right to know* about the risks we will be exposed to and obliged to endure because of the decisions of others that affect the health of the environment, and thus our own health and well-being. Knowing about and deciding upon the use of pesticides that affects us all should be everyone's right. This widespread participation in managing the environmental risks of our technological choices is still a monumental challenge for translating sustainable development into a practical reality.

> It is not my contention that chemical insecticides must never be used. I do contend that we have put poisonous and biologically potent chemicals indiscriminately into the hands of persons largely or wholly ignorant of their potentials for harm.
>
> We have subjected enormous numbers of people to contact with these poisons, without their consent and often without their knowledge. If the Bill of Rights contains no guarantee that a citizen shall be secure against lethal poisons distributed either by private individuals or by public officials, it is surely only because our forefathers, despite their considerable wisdom and foresight, could conceive of no such problem.[164]

> I contend, furthermore, that we have allowed these chemicals to be used with little or no advance investigation

of their effect on soil, water, wildlife, and man himself. Future generations are unlikely to condone our lack of prudent concern for the integrity of the natural world that supports all life.

There is still very limited awareness of the nature of the threat. This is an era of specialists, each of whom sees his own problem and is unaware of or intolerant of the larger frame into which it fits. It is also an era dominated by industry, in which the right to make a dollar at whatever costs is seldom challenged. When the public protests, confronted with some obvious evidence of damaging results of pesticide applications, it is fed little tranquilizing pills of half truth. We urgently need an end to these false assurances, to the sugar coating of unpalatable facts. It is the public that is being asked to assume the risks that the insect controllers calculate. The public must decide whether it wishes to continue on the present road, and it can do so only when in full possession of the facts. In the words of Jean Rostand, 'The obligation to endure gives us the right to know.'[165]

At the end of the book, the right to know also leads to the responsibility of deciding:

We stand now where two roads diverge . . . The road we have long been traveling is deceptively easy, a smooth superhighway on which we progress with great speed, but at its end lies disaster. The other fork of the road—the one 'less traveled by'—offers our last, our only chance to reach a destination that assures the preservation of our earth.

The choice, after all, is ours to make. If, having endured much, we have at last asserted our 'right to know', and, if knowing, we have concluded that we are being asked to take senseless and frightening risks, then we should no longer accept the counsel of those who tell us that we must fill our world with poisonous chemicals; we should look about and see what other course is open to us.[166]

The right to know also implies challenging the monopoly of experts in decision-making and risk management. Experts should give information about risks from their specific perspective, not decide about them. Risk management is a political task that should involve the public. It is up to all of us to participate in risk management through the political process, which implies integrating partial information from different specialised fields of expertise. Giving the public the ability to participate also implies a new role for scientists: they are not only the specialists who create, through the scientific method, knowledge that is highly specialised and able to solve problems by generating technological applications; they are also the ones who share knowledge and inform the public debate, thus creating real possibilities for participative decision-making in risk management. This implies a new way of communicating science to the public—an area where Carson showed total mastery.

A new role for scientists: communicating knowledge, informing the debate

Communicating science to the public also requires translating scientific (i.e. abstract and universal) knowledge into the localised knowledge of lay people.[167] In this translation (in both senses), new local (and scientific) knowledge is produced, which helps people make sense of their everyday life and create essential skills to participate in collective deliberations. This way of communicating science implies: speaking to people and not only to scientific peers (or fellow specialists); integrating several forms of specialised knowledge with local knowledge to help people develop their own worldviews, understand the meaning of things and problems they face and eventually become full citizens. Ultimately, this changes the positivist project for science, as an undertaking for the control of the world through technological applications, into a project for the creation of meaning, empowerment and full citizenship. For Carson, ecology, not chemistry, was the key science for the integrative, interdisciplinary and empowerment tasks required by this project.

In the book, it is not difficult to find examples of Carson's mastery in this new way of communicating science, which immediately establishes links to people's experiences (actual or imagined), addresses complex themes in a simple but clear and rigorous way, and uses a pedagogy of respect and wonder towards nature. This is probably one of the major strengths of the book and one of the main factors in its success. The following is an example among many:

> The trouble is that we are seldom aware of the protection afforded by natural enemies until it fails. Most of us walk unseeing through the world, unaware alike of its beauties, its wonders, and the strange and sometimes terrible intensity of the lives that are being lived about us. So it is that the activities of the insect predators and parasites are known to few. Perhaps we may have noticed on oddly shaped insect of ferocious mien on the bush in the garden and been dimly aware that the praying mantis lives at the expense of other insects. But we see with understanding eye only if we have walked in the garden at night and here and there with a flashlight have glimpsed the mantis stealthily creeping upon her prey. Then we sense something of the drama of the hunter and the hunted. Then we begin to feel something of that relentlessly pressing force by which nature controls her own.[168]

Truth, interests and economic incentives

Carson's clear perception of the interplay of truth, interests and economic incentives in the generation of scientific knowledge or its technological applications is another theme that is important in understanding some of our current dilemmas with sustainable development. Let us start with the following excerpt:

> Over the past decade these problems [the destruction of nature's resistance to pest surges] have cast long shadows, but we have been slow to recognize them.
>
> Most of those best fitted to develop natural controls and assist in putting them into effect have been too busy laboring in the more exciting vineyards of chemical control. It was reported in 1960 that only 2 per cent of all the economic entomologists in the country were then working in the field of biological controls. A substantial number of the remaining 98 per cent were engaged in research on chemical insecticides.
>
> Why should this be? The major chemical companies are pouring money into the universities to support research on insecticides. This creates attractive fellowships for graduate students and attractive staff positions. Biological-control studies, on the other hand, are never so endowed—for the simple reason that they do not promise anyone the fortunes that are to be made in the chemical industry. These are left to state and federal agencies, where the salaries paid are far less.[169]

Here, Carson does not ask herself why the industry is not making fortunes from the findings of biological control studies, like it does from the findings about chemical insecticides. This is, in part, explained because most of the knowledge about biological control (as well as most agro-ecological knowledge) has what economists call public good characteristics, which means that, once generated, this knowledge is not usually incorporated into objects that can be sold by companies (such as pesticides, genetically improved seeds or new equipment) but simply consists of available knowledge that every farmer can use to produce cheaper or better (healthier) food at a lower environmental cost. Because the input (chemicals, genetics or equipment) industry cannot sell something to capture these public benefits, it has no direct interest in them. These ideas are implicitly reflected in Carson's book:

> Dr Pickett and his associates struck out on a new road ... Recognizing that they had a strong ally in nature, they devised a program that makes maximum use of natural controls and minimum use of insecticides. Whenever insecticides are applied only minimum doses are used—barely enough to control the pest without avoidable harm to beneficial species. Proper timing also enters in. Thus if nicotine sulphate is applied before rather than after the apple blossoms turn pink one of the important predators is spared, probably because it is still in the egg stage.
>
> Dr Pickett uses special care to select chemicals that will do as little harm as possible to insect parasites and predators ... They are getting [good] results, moreover, at a substantially lower cost. The outlay for insecticides in Nova Scotia apple orchards is only from 10 to 20 per cent of the amount spent in most other apple-growing areas.[170]

Therefore, the profits from knowing about how to use pesticides, and which pesticides to use to maintain a healthier ecosystem, are made by farmers (through lower production costs today and in the future) and not by the chemical industry—which will probably endure lower sales figures. There is no new product for the industry to sell here but there is available knowledge to be used by every farmer interested in producing more cheaply and at a lower environmental cost. However, because farmers need not pay anybody to use this knowledge, the knowledge becomes a public (non-excludable) good, which does not provide private profits to industry. It is the state that should invest public money in the production of these kinds of goods. If there is no public investment, this kind of knowledge will not be available.

Vanloqueren and Baret[171] stress this different nature of knowledge produced in genetic engineering and in agro-ecological research. While the former is incorporated into private goods (e.g.

seeds) that can be sold by industry, the latter is clearly geared towards the public good (mostly related to ecological knowledge about agro-ecosystems and better management practices). This explains lower private industry funding and, consequently, the slow progress of agro-ecological research, when compared to that of genetic engineering. This is a typical example of market failure. Market failure can be corrected through public intervention, such as the investment of more public funds for agro-ecological research, in this case. Ironically, Vanloqueren's paper also reveals that governmental priorities for research funding have given greater focus to genetic engineering, in comparison to agro-ecological research. As such, research policy is exacerbating instead of correcting market failure, making agro-ecological research the poor relation of genetic engineering, in spite of the considerable potential benefits of agro-ecological research for the sustainable development of food production, in a world of limited and shrinking resources.

As explained by Carson, biased market incentives create biased interest-based statements:

> ... the otherwise mystifying fact that certain outstanding entomologists are among the leading advocates of chemical control. Inquiry into the background of some of these men reveals that their entire research program is supported by the chemical industry. Their professional prestige, sometimes their very jobs depend on the perpetuation of chemical methods. Can we then expect them to bite the hand that literally feeds them? But knowing their bias, how much credence can we give to their protests that insecticides are harmless?[172]

Conclusion: Rachel Carson's legacy for sustainable development

All the ideas discussed in the previous section constitute an implicit environmental agenda in *Silent Spring*. As suggested earlier in this chapter, they are all crucial for addressing the many challenges and dilemmas facing sustainable development today. There are still many paths to be trodden today, not only in controlling insect populations but also in many other specific domains of sustainability. This is what makes *Silent Spring* a true classic of environmental literature: it not only helped change the world in the past, it still has the potential to inspire us to change it today and in the future.

4
The Limits to Growth revisited

Tim O'Riordan

Perspective

The Limits to Growth (referred to as *Limits* from now on) in many ways epitomises the six volumes covered in this series. It initiated the era of computer-based complex modelling and the role of scenarios in assessing the future for humankind and its planetary home. It introduced the notion of limits to unending growth, and confronted humanity for the first time with the prospect of real boundaries to our endeavours. It challenged the powers of business, the military and markets to recognise the essential barriers to their hubris. It defended huge opposition and even derision by economists and systems analysts which lasted for over 30 years after its publication. It was buffeted by, but is proving resilient to, a moral credo of the ultimate triumph of the human mind and inventiveness, given suitable economic and political institutional support, to overcome all impediments of limits.

It opened the era on global environmental change and the emergence of sustainability. It resonated with the ebbs and flows of transcendentalism and the modern 'transition towns' movement. It reinforced the population debate and opened the way to tackling population as a social justice issue, not as a numbers game. It gave heart to the huge international non-governmental movements on environmental resilience, social fairness, economic redistribution, and perpetual scrutiny of environmental change, social well-being, and reliable prosperity. It created the intellectual space for interdisciplinary science, for 'sustainability science' and for participatory science. And it began the journey, in which we are only now falteringly entering, of the peaceful transition to sustainability, through revealing the essence of humanness on a unique, but ultimately unforgiving, planet.

The context

The publication of *The Limits to Growth* in March 1972, led by Dennis and Donella Meadows,[173] was explosive. In the following 30 years, it sold 12 million copies translated into 30 languages.[174] Its huge and enduring impact was due to timing, novelty, controversy and mystery. Its contemporary impact is that what its authors imagined 40 years ago is proving to be truer today than even they guessed when they wrote the volume.

Limits, as a book, well deserves recognition in this series. It is actually more powerful for the contemporary age than for its 'birth age'. The notion of 'limits' remains deeply contested in human thought and outlook. Its message openly challenged the economics profession, at the time and still today, the fiercest bastion of self-protection and political patronage. Science itself was also in the dock, as being unwilling and unable to engage with the hopes and fears of citizens. Today, 'sustainability science', which this book championed, is proving to be the supportive framework for the coming transformation.

In terms of timing, the book appeared six months before the first global mega-conference: the UN Stockholm Conference on the Human Environment, held in June 1972. This disputed event (many developing countries were deeply suspicious of the motives of the USA and European nations, seen as wishing to preserve their own growth, and China did not attend)[175] looked at the significance of pollution, waste generation and international environmental damage to forests and seas for the first time in a scientific context. It stimulated the debate over the possible environmental boundaries to continuous growth, and heralded the era of legally binding international environmental regulatory agreements. *Limits* was also an outcome of an unprecedented period of environmental 'angst', symbolised by the first Earth Day in June 1970, the passage of the US National Environmental Protection Act of 1969, and the creation of various, increasingly aggressive, national environmental protection agencies in North America and Europe. Furthermore *Limits* resonated with *The Population Bomb* by Paul and Anne Ehrlich in 1968[176] which received massive publicity. In the aftermath of the *Limits* publication was the first global oil crisis in 1973 following the Yom Kippur war, and in the following year, the cousin of *Limits,* titled *Mankind at the Turning Point* by Eduard Pestel and Mihajlo Mesarovic[177] appeared. This companion book heightened the case for complete re-evaluation of human outlooks, behaviour and governance. This case was introduced in *Limits*, but given much more prominence in subsequent versions of the initial text.[178]

The novelty was the early public use of systems dynamics modelling, an emergent tool of scenario forecasting, made more powerful by recent breakthroughs in computer technology. The particular model used in *Limits*, World3, was the brainchild of Jay Forrester, a dynamic systems engineer based in the Massachusetts Institute of Technology. Its apparent power for public opinion lay in its unfamiliarity as well as in the credence awarded by mesmeric statistics and graphics. Both *The Population Bomb* and *The Limits to Growth* were essentially scenarios, not forecasts. But in the minds of almost everyone who read these books, these charts were predictions, almost truisms; such was the power of computer-based graphics in the early 1970s. This was also a time of emerging connected science, the beginning of huge databases and associated modelling of evidence, and the (as yet) unchallenged status of international high science in national and international politics.

Almost wilful misunderstanding over possibilities rather than certainties created the controversy. Both the Ehrlich and the Meadows couples became linked to doom, despair and misjudgement. Turner[179] cites a number of well-documented critiques which virtually destroyed Meadows *et al.* in the delusional mindsets of economists, political advisers and heads of government. Both sets of authors were galvanised by a mission to turn humankind around towards what we now term 'sustainability'. This added to the cauldron of controversy, since both couples became even more obsessed by the necessity for transformation in the face of increasingly strident criticism. Yet both *Limits* and *Turning Point* are optimistic books. They chart ways of redesigning economic markets and technology, and human outlooks and cultural values. They did not seriously think we would actually reach limits of resources, but that forms of reassembled growth could be devised. So their message was optimistic. In the light of the current deepening economic malaise in the developed world, it seems that Meadows *et al.* should have been listened to 40 years ago. But the world in 1972 was not listening, as it had no ears for their message.

The mystery was the sponsorship of the *The Limits to Growth* exercise by a seemingly opaque organisation called 'the Club of Rome' headed by an Italian businessman, Aurelio Peccei, and Alexander King, a Scottish industrialist, with funding from the

Volkswagen Foundation. Peccei was boss of the Fiat automobile empire, with supposed links to right-wing transatlantic business organisations. He was very concerned about what he termed 'the predicament of mankind' and used his considerable wealth and networks to support the *Limits* modelling team.

According to the Club of Rome website, the aims of the organisation are:

> To identify the most crucial problems which will determine the future of humanity through integrated and forward-looking analysis; to evaluate alternative scenarios for the future and to assess risks, choices and opportunities; to develop and propose practical solutions to the challenges identified; to communicate the new insights and knowledge derived from this analysis to decision-makers in the public and private sectors and also to the general public and to stimulate public debate and effective action to improve the prospects for the future.[180]

This combination of a somewhat shadowy 'club', big business backing, the beginning of the global scientific modelling era, the injection of the notion of 'limits' into public anxieties over the alarming chimera of growth without end, and the onset of global political identity to the predicament of humankind, gave the book unusual force.[181]

The book

The Limits to Growth was not designed to be a prediction of doom. Yet, in the spirit of uncritical reporting, the 'inevitability' of disaster for the human race by 2100 was given almost impeccable status. Newspapers carried these typical headlines:[182] 'A computer looks ahead and shudders'; 'Study sees disaster by year 2100'; 'Scientists warn of global catastrophe'.

The notion of 'limits' carries huge significance and massive controversy. For the MIT team, composed primarily of Dennis and Donella Meadows, Jørgen Randers and William Behrens III, the model was not a prediction at all. It offered choice. It simply claimed that if there were no adjustments to a continuation of trends in population growth, in industrial output, in the use of non-renewable resources, in food production and in pollution, the most probable outcome would be a sudden and uncontrollable decline in both population and industrial capacity some time before 2100. This would lead to massive poverty, considerable human hardship and a failure of innovation.

But the book's real message was that such a wholesale calamity could be avoided if the human race altered its approach to growth by establishing a 'condition of ecological and economic stability that is sustainable far into the future'. Furthermore, such a pattern of growth, they claimed, would give every person on the planet 'basic material needs' and 'an equal opportunity to realise his or her individual human potential'.

Meadows *et al.* quoted Ralph Waldo Emerson on the notion of 'limits': 'Every nation and every man instantly surround themselves with a material apparatus which exactly corresponds to their moral state . . .'[183] Peccei went even further in his encomium for this moral state.

> The new humanism . . . must be capable of restoring within us . . . love, friendship, understanding, solidarity, as spirit of sacrifice, conviviality; and it must make us understand the more closely these qualities link us to other forms of life and to our brothers and sisters everywhere in the world, the more we shall gain.[184]

In essence, *Limits* was the first serious look at sustainable economics from the viewpoint of natural resources 'peaks', absolute food scarcity, planetary and human ill-health, and overconsumption. It was a very early call for the emergence of what is now more topical today regarding 'limits', namely: ever-increasing population, loss of ecosystem functions through disintegration of the 'web of life', and the huge social injustices of inequality or denial of personal 'flourishing'. Its value lies less in its models and scenarios, though as we shall see, these are not far off the mark, as for its precursor to the modern debate of planetary 'ceilings' and social 'floors'. *Limits* should be revisited more for its inspirational proposals for human salvation than for its graphics.

Turner summarises the strengths and weaknesses of the *Limits* World3 model:

- Interactive processes become unstable when one or more variable alters non-linearly, and can oscillate wildly if the connectivities are complex and pulsating, for example, due to the deployment of imperfect correctional measures. Many of the model runs indeed displayed these gyrating oscillations, which were endemic to the systems dynamics techniques employed, and which were conveyed into the interactions and feedbacks designed in by the mathematics.

- Finite resources, such as agricultural land, can be degraded or restored by the products of economic growth, so can be lost or enhanced for a period of time, but increase of scale or productivity comes at a progressive cost. Again, the models were essentially designed to 'crash'. This was their genre.

- Perverse outcomes of growth, such as increasing pollution, or rising death rates may be delayed, or obscured, or ignored until their damaging effects become too massive and ubiquitous to heal. Early warning may not be sensed or sought. But early warnings are almost impossible to foresee in such seemingly chaotic gyrations.

- Dealing with many sectors and variables make it very difficult to apply restorative and correctional measures in particular sectors, which do not in combination add to the perversity of chaotic and damaging outcomes. This is the notion of 'wicked problems' in the sustainability literature, when narrowly focussed institutional design in arenas such as markets, price signals, regulations, and scientific hubris, actually lead to overall worsening of human and planetary wellbeing.[185]

The World3 model was very simple. It operated on some 1,000 variables. Population was just a global figure, linked to crude birth and death rates, with no breakdown for nation or culture. Pollution was likewise an aggregated figure set on a per capita basis. For each scenario, the output presented from the model covered eight variables: global population; crude birth rate; crude death rate; services per capita; food per capita; industrial output per capita; non-renewable resources (fraction of 1900 reserves remaining); and persistent pollution (set against 1970 levels). The calculation of non-renewable resources was crudely based on existing estimates of reserves, extraction rates and substitution, but did not explicitly account for price forcing and innovation (a source of the most intense criticism by economists such as Simon[186]). Persistent pollution was the most difficult to measure, yet arguably one of the most troublesome variables, if greenhouse gases are introduced as well as non-degradable synthetic products of agriculture and industrialisation.

World3 was used to create three fundamental scenarios for a 200-year period, 1900–2100.

- *The standard run* of continued trends based on 1900–1970 data, which results in accelerating growth until the early 21st century followed by a period of sluggish growth caused by lack of available resources, diminishing agricultural productivity and increasing persistent pollution. This leads to wild oscillations and eventual collapse of population and industrial output before 2100, and possibly around 2070.

- *The comprehensive technology run* assumes a technocratic revolution of the kind envisioned by some green growth advocates, such as Ernst von Weizsäcker and Amory Lovins.[187] This was based on virtually limitless resources, 75% recycling, 25% reduction of pollution, doubling agricultural yields and widespread birth control availability. All of this merely delays the onset of collapse, which still arrives before 2100.

- *The stabilised world scenario* introduces very dramatic social and economic correctives, including universal birth control and a two-child family worldwide, huge increases in efficiency of production and pollution control, a diversion from material consumption to health and well-being, more investment in agricultural land and output sustainability, and increased lifetime of industrial capital. It is worthy of note that the Meadows team never actually preached 'zero growth', just reassembled growth.

The imagery of these model outcomes of the time was very prosaic, rather similar to a 'sepia' early photograph. The graphics showed the inevitability of overshoot and collapse in stark swooping curves. Even the stability model seemed strangely fragile and ephemeral in its floating graphics. It is easy to see why the initial readers saw these as predictions and not as explorations of simulated futures, within which lurked the somewhat simplistically programmed mathematical formulations of sincerely imperfect modelling.

In the following two decades, a number of highly critical reviews were published, helpfully summarised by Turner.[188] There were three flawed misconceptions which collectively damaged the credibility of the original book. One was the claim that *Limits* predicted a collapse of material resources before 2000, when palpably there was no such collapse. A second was the shout that humans would die out, when there was only a prediction of population declines due to higher death than birth rates. The third was that the models were inherently flawed to create preordained outcomes as desired by the particular ideology of the Club of Rome.

Here is Julian Simon, probably the most 'typical' but also the most 'thoughtful' critic of *Limits*:

> To describe those who believe that the natural resources are available in practically limitless abundance, someone has coined the phrase 'cornucopians,' to contrast with 'doomsdayers.' But please notice: The school of thought that I represent here is not cornucopian. I do not believe that nature is limitlessly bountiful. I believe instead that the possibilities in the world are sufficiently great so that with ... human imagination and human enterprise ... we and our descendants can manipulate the elements in such fashion that we can have all ... we need and desire.[189]

And here are Simon and his colleague Herman Kahn with a reaction to an official US publication *Global 2000*[190] in a prediction which brings a grim smile to the modern reader:

> Our conclusions are reassuring, though not grounds for complacency. Global problems due to physical conditions (as distinguished from those caused by institutional and political conditions) are always possible, but are likely to be less pressing in the future than in the past. Environmental, resource, and population stresses are diminishing, and with the passage of time will have less influence than now upon the quality of human life on our planet ... Because of increases in knowledge, the earth's 'carrying capacity' has been increasing throughout the decades and centuries and millennia to such an extent that the term 'carrying capacity' has by now no useful meaning. These trends strongly suggest a progressive improvement and enrichment of the earth's natural resource base, and of mankind's lot on earth.[191]

Paul Dragos Aligica summarised the Simon position very helpfully, as the Simon commentary is very important in assessing the denial of Meadows *et al.*'s initial message.

Simon went beyond criticizing various components of the neo-Malthusian paradigm. His work articulated the elements of a complex alternative social philosophy in which evolution, social exchange, and creativity play pivotal roles. Human creativity enables human beings to be different than the rest of the animal world and to create complex orders based on ideas and exchange. The institutions humans set up allow them to avoid nature's (Malthusian or neo-Malthusian) traps. Consequently the notion that nature puts a clear-cut, limiting condition on growth is a simplistic and misleading premise for public debates and governmental decisions.[192]

The concept of limits troubles society. There are many interpretations by philosophers and sociologists as to why people react so strongly to the prospect of being confined. Those who espouse liberal market economies and social order by regulation believe in the endless capacity of prices, competition and regulation to innovate and compete. They tend to be in the mainstream of politics, business, the military and international relations. They dislike the struggle of trading gains and losses, and cannot contemplate 'losing'. Those who are more egalitarian, or who less sure of the human capacity to triumph, or who empathise with a more natural rhythm (see the essays on the books by Thoreau and Schumacher in this volume), regard limits as a basis for human reflection and appropriate planetary positioning. For them, the prospect of limits is liberating and energising.

The *Limits* team were very alert to this controversy. They helpfully produced two updates, one 20 years later[193] and the other 30 years afterwards.[194] Both contained new models and up-to-date sets of data. Both reached the same conclusions. But both emphasised the crucial importance of the vital need to create a whole ethos of sustainability with the kinds of progressive institutional transformations which Emerson argued would only arise from a new moral order.

This is why *Limits* is such an important book for the modern age. It speaks neither for technological wizardry, nor for economic ecological twitching. It passionately makes the case for wholesale transformation of human values, compassion, equality of opportunity and of flourishing, and the contemporary approaches to sustainable consumption and social betterment on a global scale. All of this, which dates from the original 1972 edition, is the precursor of books such as Joseph Stiglitz's views on well-being,[195] Richard Layard's work on happiness[196] and Tim Jackson's treatise on *Prosperity without Growth*.[197] Indeed the October issue of *Resurgence*,[198] edited by our colleague Satish Kumar, is dedicated to the evolving interpretation of well-being.

The impressive accuracy of *Limits*

Graham Turner[199] offers a wonderful service to us all in reconfiguring the data used by the *Limits* team from 1970 to 2000 so as to compare the three 'runs' of the *Limits* scenarios over the 28 years following the initial publication. His findings are remarkable regarding the impressive accuracy of the 'standard run' (business as usual). For population, services per capita, food availability, industrial production and non-renewable resources reserves estimates, he found a remarkable fitting of the post-1972 *Limits* datasets. This is a powerful reproduction of both the original Forrester model as well as the prescience of the Meadows team.

Possibly of more significance is that these recent data streams do not fit at all closely with the 'stabilised world' scenario, which is the Meadows basis for sustainable development. But this particular scenario was far more affected by the inherent characteristics of the computational architecture of World3, as outlined by Turner above. Frankly, it would have been impossible to come up with credible graphics for so many interlinking assumptions as are contained in the stabilised world depiction. Nevertheless, the fact that all of the trends in the past 30 years are nowhere near simulating sustainability is very telling.

Turner puts his discovery this way:

> ... even though the comparison of scenario outputs with historical data cannot be construed as providing absolute confirmation of the model, if there were fundamental flaws in the World3 model then scenario outputs from the model would be unlikely to match the long time-series data as well as they do. This follows from the multiple interactions in the model between the demographic, industrial, agricultural, services, resources and environmental components. These interactions are likely to cause any significant flaw in one part of the model to be propagated into other outputs, resulting in multiple discrepancies with the historical data. Consequently, the good comparison of scenario outputs with historical data provides a degree of validation of the World3 model, and emphasizes the likelihood of the global system reproducing the underlying dynamics of the 'standard run' scenario.[200]

This conclusion, of course, does not mean to suggest that 'collapse and overshoot' will take place soon. Indeed, the data indicate that there is still time to adjust. So here is where Simon and Meadows share common ground, along with other commentators, such as Mark Lynas,[201] with the view that humans have the resources, imagination and collective capacity to change course. The obvious challenge is which course to take!

To begin this, we have to look at the one arena where Meadows *et al.* did not enter originally: namely, the whole theme of persistent pollution. When they wrote in 1972 there was little on the political agenda over persistent synthetic pollutants such as the organic compounds of halogens which are linked to depletion of the outer ozone layer, and the build-up of neurotoxins in blood, vital organs, the brain and sperm, though Rachel Carson (covered by José Lima Santos in this book) did identify the emergence of pesticides as a biocide in the food chain. The whole theme of the role of persistent organic pollutants is where there is still much lack of knowledge, and where the radical precepts of the precautionary principle have to be even more firmly applied.[202] Suffice it to say here that these pollutants, especially for suppression of reproductive sperm and subsequent failures of conception in humans and mammals, are by no means yet exonerated.

But where *Limits* could not reasonably have trodden lay in greenhouse gas emissions. There were greenhouse gas data in the early 1970s, of course. But the modelling sophistication of the Forrester enterprise heralded the onset of the global climate models that lie behind the whole edifice of the Intergovernmental Panel on Climate Change.[203] This is not the place to take climate change science and politics any further than its already congested domain. But it is instructive to read the latest *World Energy Outlook* of the International Energy Agency, the official UN body with the greatest clout in the energy field.

> *On planned policies, rising fossil energy use will lead to irreversible and potentially catastrophic climate change.* Global energy-related emissions of carbon dioxide (CO_2)—the principal greenhouse gas—jumped by 5.3% in 2010 to a record high of 30.4 gigatonnes (Gt). In the New Policies Scenario, our central scenario, emissions continue to rise, reaching 36.4 Gt in 2035—an increase of 20%. This trajectory is consistent with a long-term global temperature increase of more than 3.5°C.
>
> The long economic lifetimes of much of the world's energy-related capital stock mean that there is little scope for delaying action to move onto the 450 (ppmv CO_2) emissions trajectory without having to retire some stock early. We calculate that 80% of the cumulative CO_2 emitted worldwide between 2009 and 2035 in the 450 Scenario is already 'locked-in' by capital stock—including power stations, buildings and factories—that either exists now or is under construction and will still be operational by 2035, leaving little additional room for manoeuvre. If internationally co-ordinated action is not

taken by 2017, we project that all permissible emissions
in the 450 Scenario would come from the infrastructure
then existing, so that all new infrastructure from then
until 2035 would need to be zero-carbon, unless emit-
ting infrastructure is retired before the end of its economic lifetime to make headroom for new investment.
This would theoretically be possible at very high cost,
but is probably not practicable politically.[204]

This is a startling conclusion from what is traditionally a cautious organisation, with strong connections to the very industries
that are 'locking themselves into' unavoidably high carbon diox-
ide emissions. This reinforces the very 'limits' to human well-
being that Meadows *et al.* warned about 40 years ago. Ironically it
is also the product of some of the philosophies espoused by Julian
Simon and his ideological colleagues that in turn doused *Limits*
in cold delusional water in the years following its publication.

But more is to come. If we look at two aspects of the 'technological revolution' which so many economists and politicians
seek in the so-called 'green economy', we see more improbable,
yet quite scary, limits.

One lies in the availability of the 14 'rare earths' needed for
the continuation of low-carbon technologies such as solar,
wind, tidal and nuclear power, biotechnology and energy grids.
A study by the Joint Research Centre of the European Commission[205] claims that these 14 materials will require more than 1%
of world demand for these technologies, and that, of the 14, five
are likely to be in short supply by 2030. This 'bottleneck' conclusion depends on rates of extraction, the security of the supply
chains and the degree of recycling, so it is not a prediction. But
it does suggest that there may be limits to the very materials that
are urgently needed on a vast scale if the vital global low-carbon
economy is to be attained. The European Wind Energy Association[206] rebuts these conclusions by claiming that there will be sufficient of these metals for wind power generation to 2030 and that

new technology will enter by that time. The circular arguments that characterise the *Limits* concept will never die.

The other confronts precisely the wind energy association claim. This is the conclusion of an analysis, reported in *New Scientist*,[207] by Alex Kleidon of the Max Planck Institute for Biogeochemistry, shortly to be published in the *Philosophical Transactions of the Royal Society*. Kleidon argues that, if we were to replace all of our current fossil-fuelled electricity generation by wind farms, the resulting removal of the very limited 'free energy'—namely, that proportion of all energy striking the Earth that is thermodynamically usable, could be of the order of 10%. This would be sufficient to reduce the effectiveness of the usable 'natural' wind energy, and hence undermine the efficiencies of the very power-generating constructions that depend on wind power. This is because the 7 terawatt hours of replacement wind power would be sufficient to convert this fraction of free energy to unusable heat. To make matters worse, even solar voltaic panels, which depend on the limited rare earths of indium and tellurium, signposted as high-risk in the Joint Research Centre study,[208] only convert a fraction of the sunlight falling on them so also may create unusable heat.

Possibly, then, there are thermodynamic limits even to 'green technology', though this is not a theme receiving much official notice. In this context, the report of the European Climate Foundation for a low-carbon Europe-wide roadmap for 2050 dependent in part on solar and wind power and interconnected 'smart grids'[209] just may be compromised by thermodynamic limits. The Intergovernmental Panel on Climate Change 2011 report on renewable energy is also cautious about 'unlimitedness':

> In the longer term and at higher deployment levels, however, technical potentials indicate a limit to the contribution of some individual RE technologies. Factors such as sustainability concerns, public acceptance, system integration and infrastructure constraints,

or economic factors, may also limit deployment of RE technologies. [210]

Who knows: the ghost of *Limits* may reach its gnarled tentacles right into the heart of 'sustainable technology'!

One other variant of the post-1972 interpretation of limits lay in the remarkable book by Fred Hirsch (1991) titled *Social Limits to Growth*.[211] Hirsch foresaw the work of Layard on the conundrum of diminishing happiness with increased income (the *Resurgence* collection[212] covers this admirably). He argued that seeking to advance the betterment of everyone meant that everyone had to work harder just to stay in the same relative social position. His analogy was when the front row of an audience stands on tiptoe it meant that everyone behind has to rise even higher onto their tiptoes. Similarly, consumption behaviour favours the prestige of buying and enjoying goods that convey privilege and social position. So to remain socially identifiable requires the purchase of more and more expensive or rare goods, whose escalating price is founded on their uniqueness. Hirsch showed that the early limits both to consumption and to happiness lay not in natural resource scarcities or pollution, but in social envy and avarice.

On planetary boundaries and social floors

The Resilience Alliance, based in Stockholm, produced a report which may rival *Limits* as a basis for global rethinking over human limitations.[213] This group looked at nine 'planetary boundaries' which, they claim, provide the 'ceiling' for future human use of ecosystem functions and global flows of chemicals, water and energy. The seven qualities for which they felt they had access to reliable scientific information were: biodiversity; climate change; the biochemical nitrogen and phosphorus cycles; ocean acidification; stratospheric ozone; freshwater; and land use change. The two additional boundaries, where the team could not be sure of the state of evidence, were chemical pollution and atmospheric aerosol loading. They concluded that, on the themes of biodiversity, climate change and nitrogen, there was sufficient cause for claiming that these boundaries had been transgressed by the hand of humankind. Like the Meadows team, the Resilience Alliance admits the imperfections of their data and modelling, though they deployed the most sophisticated research and monitoring evidence available. They emphasise the case for more Earth systems research just to maintain better signalling of early warning.

But they do initiate a case for a completely fresh interpretation of limits.

The proposed concept of 'planetary boundaries' lays the groundwork for shifting our approach to governance and management, away from the essentially sectoral analyses of limits to growth aimed at minimising negative externalities, toward the estimation of the safe space for human development. Planetary boundaries define, as it were, the boundaries of the 'planetary playing field' for humanity if we want to be sure of avoiding major human-induced environmental change on a global scale.

We are entering possibly a new phase of the notion of limits: namely, a planetary 'ceiling' as defined by the work of the Earth system scientists, and a 'social floor' as promoted by the international developmental and civil rights organisations. Kate Raworth,[214] writing from an Oxfam perspective, introduced the notion of basic social well-being conditions which cannot be lowered if both deep-seated social injustice and possible social violence are to be avoided. These apply to basic rights of health, education, racial and gender respect, food, water, political rights to know, to assemble and to demonstrate, work and prosperity.

This creates a 'safe operating room' for human use of planetary resources, ecosystem services and human dignity. It is obvious that this 'playing space' is not fixed, as there will be lowering of the ceiling in order to raise the floor. One way to convert this challenging notion is to integrate this planetary playing space within the UN reassessment of delivering the Millennium Development Goals, which have largely stalled. This might take the form of Sustainable Development Goals, currently being explored by the Stakeholders Forum to the forthcoming UN Conference on Sustainable Development (Rio +20). This process may not prove implementable as there are many governments who are not at all keen on any hint of limits in an age of recession and considerable international economic uncertainty. For example, the British Chancellor, George Osborne, told his party conference in October 2011 that 'we're not going to save the planet by putting our country out of business' and has demanded a review, within three years, of the UK official commitments of 50% reduction in total carbon emissions by 2027, as required by the statutory Committee on Climate Change. Yet the Committee's requirements are mean to be legally binding on all UK governments.[215]

Nevertheless, the idea of a narrowing planetary playing field will not go away. It is the stuff of modern-day limits. It is also very much incorporated in the evolving examination of the economics of ecosystems and biodiversity.[216] This is also a UN-based study of the values of ecosystem processes in future economies. The notion of 'value' here applies not just to the possible costs saved by utilising the functioning of ecosystem and geo-biochemical processes in absorbing pollutants, reducing flood run-off, maintaining water availability in vegetation and ground sources, sequestering carbon in soils and forests, safeguarding critical biodiversity and reducing fire hazard. It also addresses the roles of nature in adding health and well-being to people's lives. And it tackles the spiritual and moral dimensions of being always aware of the limits of human understanding of the complete mysteries of nature. This is introduced by Aldo Leopold in the essay by Callicott in this volume. One enduring quality of nature is that humans will never fully value it, so will forever be ignorant of its true 'intrinsic-ness', and to an important extent, humbled.

Beyond *Limits*

In the 1972 edition, the *Limits* team began the discussion of what we now term sustainability:

> It is possible to alter these growth trends and to establish a condition of ecological and economic stability that is sustainable far into the future. The state of global equilibrium could be designed so that the basic needs of each person on earth are satisfied and that each person has an equal opportunity to realize her or her human potential.[217]

In the 1993 update Meadows *et al.* discussed the qualities of moral underpinning and human behaviour that will be necessary to achieve this. They suggested the following:[218]

- *Visioning what we really want*, without the constraints of reality, by identifying and pursuing dreams. Quoting the Emerson dictum, they claim that 'vision, when widely shared and firmly kept in sight, *brings into being new systems*'. They foresee the new limits of safe playing fields; of honest leaders; of the art of living; of dignity in economic activity which builds human potentialities; and of building social enterprise and personal self-esteem so that all people become citizens with a deep sense of sensitised compassion.

- *Networking through empathetic sharing* and productive negotiation through open-mindedness and flexible responsiveness. Networks create action at all levels of social and economic life. They are the essence of 'positive deviation', the capacity to change by leading from the unfamiliar but through the grain of society, not from the top.[219]

- *Truth telling by avoiding deliberate distortion*, and by admitting that we will always ultimately be wrong if we continue to pursue the same course to which we are currently committed, by which we are almost blinded.

- *Learning by creating scope for crossing the boundaries of the familiar* and addressing the excitement of novelty and new partnerships; of experimental institutional arrangements in regulation, financing, measuring and marketing; by creating an exhilarating conversation between all of the sciences; by embracing the public sentiment, and by recognising failure as a bonus in the curve of learning.

- *Loving by generosity*, by nurturing others, by unconditionality of action, and by exhibiting patience.

These observations echo the views of all of the other authors of the books reviewed in this collection. This is why *Limits* helps to bind and to reveal. The only serious limits are the limits of not trying out these precepts; of being imprisoned by accustomed outlooks and beliefs which are buttressed by the fear of letting go of the very failings that are drawing us inexorably into limits.

Maybe the greatest legacy of *Limits* is for us all to believe collectively that our only limits are to accept what we have fatally fashioned already for ourselves; and that there are no limits to our transcendental transformation should we conscientiously follow the Meadows precepts.

5
Small is still beautiful

Satish Kumar

E.F. Schumacher was a champion of the Green Economy. He advocated smallness because it was compatible with greenness. Giant factories engaged in mass production and giant corporations engaged in mass transportation naturally lead to the pollution of land, air and water, depletion of resources and destruction of human creativity. That is why Schumacher came to the conclusion that small is not only beautiful; it is also necessary and essential even if it is not enough or sufficient. Small is necessary because it provides a potential for people to be spontaneous, creative, flexible and innovative. At a smaller scale we are much better disposed to exercise a greater degree of autonomy and to improve existing plans and rules according to changing circumstances. Moreover we are better able to care for our environment.

In 1962 Rachel Carson had presented a scientific case for a greater understanding and care of the natural environment.

In 1972 the UN had organised its first environmental conference in Stockholm, attended by many heads of state and government leaders, where a strong political case was made for a change of policy in favour of environmental protection. At the time the Club of Rome had also published its seminal research under the title of *The Limits to Growth*, which made a strong plea for shifting the focus from consumption to conservation.

All this was very encouraging. But Schumacher felt that unless we challenge the 'religion of economics' the science and politics of environment was not enough. The world was gripped by a system of economics that was anti-people and anti-natural. He had written a number of essays laying the foundation of an ecological economics. Inspired by the work of Rachel Carson, the UN conference in Stockholm and *The Limits to Growth*, he set down to weave his essays together into a book. The result was *Small is Beautiful*.

But to begin with it was not easy and the book did not become an instant classic. When Schumacher sought a publisher for the book, it proved an uphill task. Publisher after publisher sent him a note saying 'no thank you'. In the end a small publisher (also perhaps a crank!) spotted the potential of the book, which was originally titled *Homecomers: Economics as if People Matter*.

Having read the manuscript Anthony Blond said to Schumacher: 'What you are really talking about is that smallness is a prerequisite for human happiness and well-being, for social cohesion and environmental caring, for peace and for freedom.'

Schumacher replied, 'Yes, you are right, I am saying that but I am saying much more than that!'

Blond suggested, 'Why not call your book *Small is Beautiful*, and make *Economics as if People Matter* the subtitle. The title of the book needs to be snappy, short and memorable.'

Schumacher liked the idea because for him Beauty was as important, if not more so, as Smallness. Small by itself is no guarantee of goodness. Small also has to be beautiful and good.

Therefore getting these two words and two concepts into one title with simplicity and accessibility was an attractive proposition. Schumacher said to Anthony, 'I like it; as you are the publisher and if you think that your title will sell the book then I am happy to agree.'

Anthony Blond was pleased and published the book in hardback in 1973. As Schumacher had had difficulty in finding a publisher, so Blond had difficulty in marketing it. The British media and the market found the book too idealistic and Utopian. However, Blond was successful in getting the book published in the United States where it resonated with the media and academia. Schumacher went on a book tour of the length and breadth of the USA and spoke to packed audiences in universities, churches and town halls. Somehow Jerry Brown, the then Governor of California, got hold of a copy. He read it and was so inspired that he invited Schumacher to the governor's house. Talking to him personally was even more exhilarating and impressive—so much so that Brown phoned Jimmy Carter and insisted that the President meet him. Schumacher being invited to the White House became big news in the UK and suddenly the media, MPs, academics and booksellers in his homeland rediscovered him and the book became a bestseller. Soon it was translated into most of the world's major languages! Now by everybody's acclaim the book became a green classic. In this essay I will attempt to describe the salient points of this groundbreaking book.

Organisations are conceived and built for some ideals such as caring for the health of others, or providing education for the young, or producing and distributing food for communities. Large-scale organisations tend to get bogged down in the maintenance of the organisation itself, and the ideals for which an organisation was set up easily become secondary. Large scale often forces people to be at the service of the organisation, whereas small scale tends to put the organisation at the service of the people.

One of the primary tests of an organisation is whether it turns people into instruments to perpetuate the system and sees people as a means to an end, or whether the organisation exists as a means and people are the end. Large business organisations particularly aim to maximise profit and people become subservient to the profit motive, whereas smaller business organisations are better able to maintain a balance between the well-being of their members and the community they serve and their impact on the natural world, while still keeping an eye on the bottom line.

Similarly, large government organisations become obsessed with their hold on power. Other human, social and ecological considerations become subsidiary to the overriding imperative of remaining in control even if lip service is paid to improving public services or maintaining sustainable development.

Schumacher wrote:

> there always appears to be a need for at least two things simultaneously ... freedom and order. We need the freedom of lots and lots of small autonomous units and at the same time the orderliness of large scale ... when it comes to action we need small units because action is a highly personal affair and one cannot be in touch with more than a very limited number of persons at any one time.[220]

While Schumacher and other decentralist thinkers advocated the paramount importance of human scale, this was mainly a matter of physical organisations and not any kind of parochial, narrow or nationalist confinement. Schumacher himself agreed that 'when it comes to the world of ideas, to principles or ethics, to the indivisibility of peace and ecology we need to recognise the unity of human kind'.

Without any doubt we are members of the Earth community and all national, political, religious and industrial boundaries are of secondary importance. We need to recognise the sacredness and intrinsic value of all life without confining ourselves to any sectional or sectarian interest. But we are limited by our physical stature and therefore we are able to form active and personal relationships with only a few people. The whole Earth is our home and yet we develop a sense of place and a spiritual connection with the place where we actually live. Smallness is not to be confused with narrowness. The idea of small was not a matter of dogmatic belief for Schumacher. He often spoke of appropriate scale. However he was highlighting the importance of smallness because he found the world obsessed with 'an almost universal idolatry of giantism'; therefore he found it necessary to insist on the virtues of smallness. 'If there were a prevailing idolatry of smallness', Schumacher wrote, 'one would have to try and exercise influence in the opposite direction'. Schumacher further explained that 'For every activity there is a certain appropriate scale'.

Scale of human settlements

Not only do political, social or business organisations need to be built at an appropriate scale, but human settlements also must be planned on the principle of human scale. The mindless growth of cities around the world worried Schumacher enormously. 'Millions of people start moving about, deserting the rural areas and the smaller towns to follow the city lights, to go to the big city causing a pathological growth.'[221] Schumacher was concerned about the creation of megalopolises where tens of millions of people converge, creating congestion, pollution and alienation, losing community, beauty and simplicity.

For Schumacher the upper limit of a desirable city was about half a million inhabitants. In such a small city, citizens are able to walk from one end to the other without needing to get into a car or a bus. A citizen is able to access school, shops, library, theatre, clinic and other amenities on foot. There is a better balance between city and country; nature and culture live side by side. Such a city should be surrounded by farms, fields and orchards which can supply the city's needs with the minimum of transportation. Energy should be derived from sun, wind, water and wood. Even a little bit of fossil fuel goes a long way if frugality and a no-waste policy becomes an integral part of city culture. Allotments, roof gardens, water harvesting can all be possible in the city because people live together within the context of mutuality, cooperation and care.

Schumacher explained:

> The all-pervading disease of the modern world is the total imbalance between city and countryside, an imbalance in terms of wealth, power, culture, attraction, and hope. The former has become over-extended and the latter has atrophied. The city has become the universal magnet, while rural life has lost its savour. Yet it remains an unalterable truth that, just as a sound mind depends on a sound body so the health of the cities depends on the health of the rural areas. The cities, with all their wealth, are merely secondary producers, while primary production, the precondition of all economic life, takes place in the countryside. The prevailing lack of balance, based on the age-old exploitation of countryman and raw material producer, today threatens all countries throughout the world, the rich even more than the poor. To restore a proper balance between city and rural life is perhaps the greatest task in front of modern man. It is not simply a matter of raising agricultural yields so as to avoid world hunger. There is no answer to the evils of mass unemployment and mass migration into cities, unless the whole level of rural life can be raised, and this requires the development of an agro-industrial culture, so that each district, each community, can offer a colourful variety of occupations to its members.[222]

Economy of scale

Small scale naturally leads to a local economy as large scale leads to globalisation, which is wholly dependent on excessive and wasteful use of fossil fuel, requiring massive infrastructure and mindless mobility.

Once Schumacher noticed a lorry full of biscuits coming from Edinburgh to London and a little later he learnt that lorries carry biscuits from London to Edinburgh. As an economist he failed to see the point of why able and creative human beings are compelled to drive lorries for hours on end going from Edinburgh to London and from London to Edinburgh carrying biscuits at huge cost to the environment. Surely the Scottish recipes for biscuits could be learnt by London bakers and vice versa, avoiding air pollution, human boredom and road construction. After much thought and analysis Schumacher could not work out the economic logic of this transaction so he consoled himself jokingly, 'Oh well, I am a mere economist and not a nutritionist, perhaps by transporting biscuits over long distances the nutritional content of the biscuits is increased!'

Not only biscuits but even water is transported long distances. Once I saw Scottish Highland Water being sold in a French supermarket and French water in Scotland. I wondered why Scottish water is not good enough for the Scots and French water for the French. Of course when there is trade between Scottish whiskey and French Cognac one can see the logic: that is proper trade. But what is the point of exporting and importing water?

Britain exports almost an equal amount of butter as she imports. The same is true with many other products. Schumacher was one of the first to point out the senselessness and stupidity of such a system.

In the name of the economy of scale we ignore the diseconomies of scale. While millions of people in Europe and the United States have no work and are forced to live on social benefits, goods are imported from China which could easily be made locally, providing work, reducing pollution and liberating these countries from the enormous burden of debt.

Psychology of scale

Small scale is also conducive to psychological and emotional well-being. In large-scale organisations the integrity of the individual is often lost. The individual feels 'nothing more than a small cog in a vast machine when human relationships of daily working life become increasingly dehumanised',[223] wrote Schumacher. Large-scale organisations are more concerned with efficiency and productivity, and the place of human happiness and spiritual fulfilment does not figure. Schumacher further explained,

> Nobody really likes large scale organisations; nobody likes to take orders from a superior who takes orders from another superior. Even if the rules devised by bureaucracy are humane nobody likes to be ruled by rules, that is to say, by people whose answer to every complaint is, 'I did not make the rules; I am merely applying them'.[224]

People in large organisations do like orderliness but that orderliness is often static and lifeless, and individuals within these organisations often lack a sense of adventure and the courage to take risks. Schumacher believed that the ideal organisation is that where there is 'plenty of elbow room and scope for breaking through the established order to do the things never done before, never anticipated by the guardians of orderliness'. Schumacher cherished creativity where an 'unpredicted and unpredictable outcome' is encouraged. Schumacher saw:

> the specific danger inherent in large scale organisation was its natural bias and tendency in favour of order at the expense of creative freedom ... the man of order is

typically the accountant and the administrator; while
the man of creative freedom is the entrepreneur. Order
requires intelligence and is conducive to efficiency;
while freedom calls for, and opens the door to, intuition
and leads to innovation . . . without the magnanimity of
disorder venturing into the unknown and incalculable,
without the risk and the gamble, the creative imagination rushing in where bureaucratic angels fear to tread—
without this, life is a mockery and a disgrace.[225]

Ecology of scale

If economic activities are conducted at a small and local level
then it follows that the human footprint on the Earth will also
be small. Large-scale mass production gives rise to large-scale
mass consumption, leading to large-scale waste and pollution,
whereas small-scale, local and mindful production by the masses
will result in careful consumption, incorporating the ideals of
reducing, reusing, repairing and recycling the objects and goods
of daily use.

Schumacher's concern for smallness was not small for its own
sake but he believed that small is sustainable and environmentally friendly. Modern society committed to a large-scale capitalist system looks at nature merely as a resource for maximising
profit.

Classical economics was built on three fundamental principles:
land, labour and capital. Land represented all natural resources
overground as well as underground. The land had intrinsic value.
It was not merely a commodity to buy and sell. Labour represented people and they were not merely instruments of making
profit. Economics was there for the well-being and welfare of land
and people. Capital had a place but it was in the third position
and its function was to facilitate the right relationship between
land and labour.

But modern economics has turned the three principles upside down. Capital has become the domineering master. In this model land and labour exist to serve capital. In classical economics the true wealth was land, forests, animals, minerals, rivers, human ingenuity, creativity and skills. Capital was there to oil the wheels. In modern economics financial capital, or money, has become the wealth, whereas money should be considered merely a measure of wealth, a means of exchange and not wealth itself. This primacy of money in the economic model is the cause of the environmental crisis.

The mission of the modern economy is to maximise profit and the method is to dominate and conquer nature. Industrialists talk of a battle with nature—the way they treat nature is as if they were at war with her. Factory farming, genetic engineering, industrialisation of ploughing and harvesting, the use of fertilisers, pesticides and herbicides, clear-cutting of forests, opencast mining, deep drilling in search of oil, industrial scale of fishing and umpteen other examples are evidence of the fact that the industrial economy sees nature to be fought and won. The captains of modern economy are unaware of the fact that even if they win the war they will find themselves on the losing side.

Schumacher considered nature to be the true capital, defining the word in its broadest meaning. He insisted that we should conserve, safeguard and protect natural capital for her own sake and for the sake of future generations. Respect and reverence for the intrinsic value of sacred nature Schumacher called 'meta economics'. He wrote:

> Fossil fuels are merely a part of the natural capital which we steadfastly insist on treating as expendable, as if it were income. If we squander our fossil fuels, we threaten civilisation; but if we squander the capital represented by living nature around us, we threaten life itself.[226]

If we are faithful to classical economics then we will consume the gifts of nature with modesty and moderation and for the satisfaction of our vital needs and not for the gratification of our greed. Schumacher agreed with Mahatma Gandhi that 'There is enough in the world for everybody's need but not enough for anybody's greed.'

The industrial and capitalist economy recklessly squanders natural capital 'as if it were something we had made ourselves and could easily replace out of our much-vaunted and rapidly rising productivity'.[227]

In Schumacherian economics, the aim is to create 'health, beauty and permanence and learn to live peacefully, not only with our fellow humans but also with nature'. In capitalist economics the aim is to pursue continuous and unlimited economic growth, which Schumacher called pathological and which he considered to be an impossibility, because one cannot have unlimited or infinite growth on a finite Earth.

Spirituality and scale

The single-minded pursuit of economic growth is pure materialism in which greed is systematically cultivated and restraint, frugality and wisdom have no place. According to Schumacher we have become far too clever

> to be able to survive without wisdom . . . the exclusion of wisdom from economics was something which we could perhaps get away with for a little while, as long as we were relatively unsuccessful; but now that we have become very successful the problem of spiritual and moral truth moves into the central position.[228]

Schumacher again and again highlights the essential connection between economics and wisdom. He wrote:

The cultivation and expansion of needs is the antithesis of wisdom, it is also the antithesis of freedom and peace. Every increase of needs tends to increase one's dependence on outside forces over which we cannot have control, and therefore increases existential fear. Only by a reduction of needs can one promote a genuine reduction in those tensions which are the ultimate causes of strife and war.[229]

Large-scale economics is the economics of war and violence:

Ever bigger machines, entailing ever bigger concentrations of economic power and exerting ever greater violence against the environment, do not represent progress: they are a denial of wisdom. Wisdom demands a new orientation of science and technology towards the organic, the gentle, the non violent, the elegant and beautiful. Peace is indivisible—how then could peace be built on a foundation of reckless science and violent technology?[230]

wrote Schumacher.

It was for peace, sustainability and well-being of people and the Earth that Schumacher advocated small-scale organisations because he believed that they will always be less harmful to the natural environment and less likely to lead to war than large-scale ones.

Schumacher was aware of the fact that even small communities can be guilty of destruction and aggression, but because of their limited scale their impact will also be small in comparison with the negative impact that gigantic groups or nations, motivated by power, profit and greed exert. If there was any evidence that bigness will be accompanied by humility, modesty and restraint then he would have had no objection to large-scale operations, corporations and nations. But that, he believed, is not the case.

Having been through the experience of working with large organisations Schumacher saw that big organisations make their judgements on a very narrow basis and these judgements are biased towards the short term: quarterly balance sheets or the annual profit margin. Moreover, transnational corporations seeking global markets depend on the infrastructure built by governments with taxpayers' money and yet they are able to employ clever accountants to avoid paying taxes. Further, their financial calculations exclude the true cost to the environment.

In addition to narrowness and short-termism, large economic institutions encourage irresponsible individualism; they are not concerned with spiritual, social and environmental well-being. They will consider it uneconomic, for example, to give preference to locally produced goods if imported goods are cheaper. Market forces, free trade, globalisation and economic growth put together have created the 'religion of economics' where the reign of quantity triumphs. Schumacher wrote, 'When economic thinking is based on the market, it takes the sacredness out of life, because there can be nothing sacred in something that has a price'.[231] In such a system, even simple non-economic values like beauty, health or cleanliness can survive only if they prove to be 'economic'.

Buddhist economics

Schumacher was invited by the Burmese government to advise them on developing their economy on the Western model. In 1955, he spent nearly six months in Burma visiting villages, towns, temples, monasteries and talking to wise elders. He soon realised that the Burmese had a perfectly good economics of their own which he called Buddhist Economics. At that time he could see that the ordinary Burmese were contented, creative and close to nature, happily caring for the land, animals and people. Of course they could develop a few intermediate and appropriate technologies to ease their work but why should an industrial, urban and mechanised system be imposed on them?

It became clear to him that replacing such a traditional economy with a modern Western-style economy would lead to more problems than solutions. He realised that Buddhists see 'the essence of civilisation not in a multiplication of wants but in the purification of human character'. And that character is partly formed by good work and the dignity of labour. For Schumacher work was not merely a job, an occupation or employment. It was a source of creativity, imagination and spiritual growth; 'work properly conducted ... blesses those who do it and equally their products', wrote Schumacher. Through good work, what the Buddhists call 'Right Livelihood', human beings are transformed for the better and through bad work they are transformed for the worse. Therefore society has an obligation to encourage good work and to value its artisans, artists, craftspeople, farmers, gardeners, builders and traders. The industrialisation of work and mass production diminishes the opportunity for good work and therefore 'purification of human character'. Good work is not to be confused with drudgery. Good work and good living complement each other. Good work improves the quality of life and brings general well-being.

Buddhism is not 'antagonistic to physical well-being', Schumacher wrote, 'It is not wealth that stands in the way of liberation but the attachment to wealth; not the enjoyment of pleasurable things but craving for them. The keynote of Buddhist economics, therefore, is simplicity and non-violence.'[232] The Buddhist economist would say that:

> since consumption is merely a means to human well-being the aim should be to obtain the maximum of well-being with the minimum of consumption ... and [since] physical resources are everywhere limited, people satisfying their needs by means of a modest use of resources are obviously less likely to be at each other's throats than people depending upon a high rate of use. Equally people who live in highly self-sufficient local communities are less likely to get involved in large-

scale violence than people whose existence depends on worldwide systems of trade.[233]

Moreover, 'to satisfy human wants from far away sources rather than sources nearby signifies failure rather than success'.[234]

Thus Schumacher found his discovery of Buddhist economics a homecoming. Schumacher found abhorrent the idea that the industrialisation of agriculture is development, and living by the land and obtaining a livelihood through small-scale agriculture with the help of craftwork and human-scale trade is underdevelopment. The pursuit of pure materialism, for Schumacher, was a dead end. Integrating the Buddhist principles of small, simple and non-violent way of life with principles of sound economies will facilitate a spiritually, socially and ethically resilient society. He came to the view that his task and that of his generation was one of 'metaphysical reconstruction'.

This conviction was not merely an emotional response. It was based on intellectual and empirical evidence that modern industry swallows so much of natural resources while accomplishing very little. Schumacher wrote:

> An industrial system which uses 40% of the world's primary resources to supply less than 6% of the world's population (of the rich countries) could be called efficient only if it obtained strikingly successful results in terms of human happiness, well-being, culture, peace and harmony.[235]

It was self-evident to Schumacher that the economically developed countries like the USA and Europe had not achieved the desired success in environmental sustainability, social coherence or human happiness, whereas a country like Burma, which had a flourishing democracy at that time, and was mostly agrarian with thriving craftsmanship and great adherence to the Buddhist principles of simplicity and non-violence, was much happier and less demanding of natural resources.

Schumacher was one of the rare economists from the Western world who saw the intrinsic link between economics and ethics. Buddhism for him was a metaphor for moral and spiritual values. He wanted society to follow the direction of non-violence rather than violence, cooperation with nature rather than her destruction, low-energy solutions rather than the brutal, wasteful and clumsy solutions of fossil-fuel-driven, nuclear-power-based industrial societies. Schumacher was convinced that a way of life that bases itself on materialism, on limitless expansionism of economy in a finite environment, cannot last long.

Explaining his view of a Buddhist economics, he wrote that it:

> would make the distinction between 'renewable' and 'non-renewable' resources. A civilisation built on renewable resources, such as the products of forestry and agriculture, is by this fact alone superior to one built on non-renewable resources, such as oil, coal, metal, etc. This is because the former can last, while the latter cannot last. The former co-operates with nature, while the latter robs nature. The former bears the sign of life, while the latter bears the sign of death. It is already certain beyond the possibility of doubt that the 'oil-coal-metal-economies' cannot be anything else but a short abnormality in the history of humankind. The New Economics would be a veritable 'Statute of Limitation'—and that means a Statue of 'Liberation'.[236]

Again and again he emphasised that 'Economics is not an exact science; it is in fact, or ought to be, something much greater: a branch of wisdom'. He came to the conclusion that life, including economics, is worth living, only if it is an unpredictable, unfolding, an emerging process and a pilgrimage.

Schumacher's pilgrimage

He began his own pilgrimage by escaping from Nazi Germany in 1937. While his brother-in-law Werner Heisenberg, the quantum physicist, decided to stay in Germany, Schumacher declared that the fight against Nazism could only be conducted outside Germany. So he came to live in England. But as fate would have it he became an alien suspect and therefore was interned. Then his friend David Astor, the owner and editor of the *Observer* newspaper, offered him a house on his land and some work on the farm. This was the beginning of his journey of deep appreciation and affinity with the natural world. He felt totally at ease working with his hands, cultivating the soil, caring for the animals and being out in nature—be it wind, rain or snow. Here was an Oxford economist getting his hands dirty in the soil, which eventually led him to becoming the president of the Soil Association, campaigning for organic agriculture and tender loving care of plants, trees, animals and all living creatures.

Eventually he himself acquired a four-acre garden in Caterham, south of London, and devoted himself to the growing of vegetables, herbs, flowers and fruit trees. His love of silviculture made him a keen advocate of the regeneration of forests. His film *On the Edge of the Forest* was a profound statement of the unity between nature and humankind. He firmly believed that in order to cultivate respect and reverence for nature it is important to shift our consciousness from ownership to relationship. We do not own land, forests, animals or rivers; we are merely temporary custodians of the natural resources under our care. We must recognise their intrinsic value. Our duty and responsibility is to take care of them without polluting, depleting or exhausting them.

'An ounce of practice is worth more than a ton of theory', he said. And therefore he practised what he preached. He was a conservationist, an ecologist, protector of wildlife and a promoter of organic agriculture. But above all he lived his ideals in his everyday life.

His farmer friend, Sam Mayall, also a member of the Soil Association, supplied him with organically grown wheat. 'I want to know exactly where my food is coming from', he said. He had his own small flourmill to grind his own flour. He baked bread every week for the family. The fruit, vegetables and herbs came from his own garden which he cultivated with profound devotion. He fed the soil with compost he had made. He believed that 'If you take care of the soil, the soil will take care of the rest.'

Schumacher was an Oxford economist, the head of statistics of the UK National Coal Board, and a member of a highly scientific and intellectual family. Yet he was attracted to Buddhism, environmentalism, baking, gardening, windmills and solar power. This was in the 1960s and 1970s, when such things were considered to be fringe and flaky. People found him rather odd. They called him a crank. Schumacher retorted, 'What's wrong with being a crank? A crank is a small and simple tool which causes revolutions.' His book *Small is Beautiful* proved to be revolutionary. It revolutionised the hearts and minds of many millions.

Schumacher's legacy

I met Schumacher in 1968 when I was running the London School of Non-Violence. Schumacher spoke there on economics of non-violence. In 1973, as his book was in the process of being published, I was offered the editorship of *Resurgence* magazine by its founder, John Papworth, I was in two minds: to accept or not to accept the honour. While talking to Schumacher about it, he spotted my hesitation,

> 'What's the problem? You will be an excellent editor', said Schumacher.

'But I would like to go back to India', I said.

'Why?'

'I would like to continue working with the Gandhians.'

'Satish, there are many Gandhians in India, we need one in England, so why not accept this offer and make *Resurgence* a voice of Gandhian philosophy in the West,' said Schumacher.

This was a very persuasive argument. My hesitation melted away.

'Alright, I will accept the editorship at your advice but I will need your support. Will you undertake to write an article for every issue?' I asked.

'OK, that's the deal', was Schumacher's reply.

I was delighted. Schumacher kept his promise until he died in 1977. The collection of his 35 *Resurgence* essays are now published as a book entitled *This I Believe*.

Four years of working relationship with Schumacher developed into a profound friendship. Whenever I received his article I would phone him and talk about it. Often we would discuss ideas and themes for the magazine as well as philosophy, politics, religion and much more.

When Schumacher died in 1977 I felt that although he has passed away physically, his vision and values will inspire generations to come. It is a sacred responsibility of his friends to keep his vision alive, develop it further and bring it to the attention of the public in general and the emerging environmental movement in particular.

With this commitment and passion I called a meeting of a number of his friends and environmentalists and we established the Schumacher Society, Annual Schumacher Lectures held in

Bristol (1977), the Small School in Hartland (1982) for education of children aged 11–16 years, Human Scale Education Movement to support small innovative schools, and eventually in 1991 Schumacher College for the study of ecological and spiritual values and for transformative learning.

Thus the work and legacy of Schumacher in the UK is flourishing. Similar societies were established in the United States, Germany and India. The work of the Intermediate Technology Development Group of which Schumacher was the founder is going on from strength to strength under the new name Practical Action, operating in many countries at the grassroots level, promoting sustainable, holistic and ecological development. Similarly, the work of the Soil Association of which Schumacher was the president is a continuous expression of this approach to land and farming. The work of the New Economics Foundation, the Centre for Alternative Technology and Friends of the Earth brings Schumacher's approach into the arena of policy and influencing the political landscape in the UK and around the world. And of course *Resurgence* magazine is the flagship publication of Schumacherian philosophy, articulating a holistic vision through art, poetry and essays on politics, economics, ecology and ethics.

At a time when the world is facing some acute global crises such as global warming, global poverty, global debt and a widespread moral vacuum, simple solutions proposed by Schumacher may be our salvation: think small, go local and act from a high moral ground. That is what Schumacher meant by metaphysical reconstruction. The time is ripe for this and the time is now. Let us take up the challenge.

6

An essay on
Our Common Future

Marina Silva

On 31 December 1987, after many public hearings and meetings in various parts of the globe; after studying around 500 written documents from several countries and mobilising the attention of global society and governments, the World Commission on Environment and Development, chaired by Norway's Gro Harlem Brundtland, ceased its activities, sure in the knowledge that it had produced something important for humanity. Debated and quoted many thousands of times since then and unanimously considered as a diagnostic milestone regarding the state of the complex relationships between humanity and its natural environment, the result of this commission's work instituted the concept of sustainable development as a kind of macro-perspective through which the solutions for extreme environmental degradation required at the time (and still required) should focus.

Today, almost 25 years later, *Our Common Future* (or the Brundtland Report) remains fresh and stimulating, its content affecting the way we understand the intersection between society and the environment, between economics and ecology.

Because of the importance of its work, the magnitude of the proposals it debated and presented, as well as the controversy it aroused and still arouses to this day, the Commission gave the Report the suggestive and challenging title *Our Common Future*; a title that says a great deal, by proposing the breaking of objective and subjective boundaries, while highlighting the realisation that, beyond geopolitics, cultures, language and ethnic barriers, there is something that unites and threatens every one of the planet's inhabitants; by asserting that the environmental crisis resulting from predominant lifestyles and development in the world can only be resolved using a paradigm of solidarity: something bigger than differences and conflicts and beyond vested powers and interests.

According to *Our Common Future*, the environmental crisis is essentially a crisis of civilisation.

The Commission spent four years in an intense process of discussion and mobilisation. At each of the events, the content of the final document was being defined via the presentation of problems, proposals for solutions, creative approaches, in-depth analyses and, most of all, through the invaluable exchange of ideas among human beings who were so different and yet so united in their desire to see the future in a way that was different and more suited to the complex situation that we face.

Gro Brundtland, who was nominated Chairman by the Secretary-General of the United Nations, had Mansour Kalid, from Sudan, as her vice-chairman, and both chose the remaining members of the Commission, who participated as citizens of the world and not as representatives of their own countries. The proposal was to free themselves from institutional constraints, economic and social interests and their distinctive cultural backgrounds to make a contribution to humanity, in the interest of preserving the planet.

This directive undoubtedly played an important role in the nature of the document and the progress of global environmental governance in recent decades, when it established this ethical milestone as a common guide for action and interaction. Unfortunately, it has not been totally assimilated, particularly by those who make decisions on a global level; however, it is undeniable that *Our Common Future* set the tone in 1992 for the Rio-92 Conference on Environment and Development, and it was also influential in the genesis and organisation of three major conventions: the Convention to Combat Desertification, the Convention on Biological Diversity and the Convention on Climate, as well as various protocols and a series of structures that are part of the system of global environmental governance we have today.

By refusing to deal with the environment in isolation, on the insistence of its Chairman, the Commission established an issue approach model that focused not only on environmental issues *per se* but also on their role as part of the development process. In the same way, neither could the environmental and energy crises of the 1980s be seen as separate from the structural fabric of the development model of the time.

The known forms of development, which simultaneously led to increasingly rapid environmental decline and social iniquities, needed to be overcome. The Report is emphatic in highlighting that challenge as a structural turning point for all societies throughout the world. That fundamental message questioned established mental models and showed the way forward, making explicit the tasks that are still on the agenda of nations and world leaders as unfinished homework.

At that time, Gro Brundtland's vision and firm position prevented the work drifting towards a mechanical and fragmented approach, anticipating the unprecedented integration that would occur in the world in the decades that would follow, with globalisation making economies and markets interconnected in such a way that we can virtually say they are common. The other side of that integration is the environmental crisis, particularly in relation to climate, which dramatically highlights that general interdependence and interconnection. As a result of this, social justice, social inclusion, national security, human rights and the rights of future generations also become global problems whose solutions can no longer be devised merely at the isolated level of each individual country.

The Commission was created to make a purposeful diagnosis of the serious problems ravaging the natural bases of development that had been identified since the 1960s and which had worsened in the 1970s and 1980s. Despite the need to update the data and specific issues raised, the results are extremely relevant from the perspective of the vision, concepts and values they contain. The Report can be considered a kind of thread via which we can interpret the current global environmental crisis, being very contemporary in that respect. At the same time, it has already become a classic: a classic of economic sustainability, social sustainability, environmental sustainability and cultural sustainability. That dual character, both classic and contemporary, makes *Our Common Future* one of the products of human intelligence that maintains the validity of its statements for a very long time.

After the Report was published, the UN began to take on board the idea of sustainable development, understanding it as a dynamic process that should be part of the different facets of human societies. It also provided a very interesting platform to analyse it when it established four constituent dimensions of the idea of sustainability: environmental, economic, social and cultural.

The first of these dimensions tells us that, to be considered sustainable, development needs to be so from an environmental perspective. According to the concepts contained in the Report, this means using natural resources, while strictly observing the support capacity of ecosystems, in order to meet the real needs of contemporary populations without compromising the rights of those who will come after. The expression *real needs* focuses attention on the fact that needs are historical and cultural constructs; however, there are basic needs, such as food, housing and opportunities to fulfil one's potential, which, although they have manifested themselves in different forms in every era and culture, span time, carrying with them their universal nature that is inextricable from the human condition itself, without adjectives.

In terms of economic sustainability, the model considered sustainable is that which transforms natural resource bases into comparative advantages and, later, into economic gains. In addition to this, sustainability in this area requires global organisations to be concerned with helping countries in several of the world's regions, whose poorer and more vulnerable populations still lack access to good public services in the areas of health, education and housing. To this end, economic sustainability is a process that has its own internal dynamic associated with dynamics geared towards the outside world, such as social ethics, the distribution of wealth and the creation of real, stable opportunities, so that people can live well without compromising natural resources or exhausting them.

The social sustainability dimension adopted by the UN establishes the principle of equity, in which economic activities and the use of natural resources take on the role of improving people's quality of life. It implies applying the principle of social equality without diluting individual differences and creating opportunities where each individual can develop their own abilities, most of all through education, quality health care and decent housing. It is those public policies that transform wealth into quality of life, not ignoring the word for the soul as an integral part of the bread for the body.

However, when we think of today, it is obvious that this is an aspect of sustainability that we are far from achieving, given that there are around 2 billion human beings who survive on less than two dollars a day. Of those 2 billion, 16 million are in my country, Brazil. Successive Brazilian politicians have made continued efforts and, with major support from society, we have lifted 25 million people out of poverty in the last eight years. That result occurred thanks to the progress of internally coherent economic and social policies which have been implemented over the last 16 years, despite there being two different parties in government.

There can be no satisfaction with the idea of social, environmental and economic sustainability alone. The idea of cultural sustainability is flagged in the Report, as well as being part of the United Nations' activities and global environmental governance. A development model is sustainable when it is capable of respecting differences; when it is able to preserve cultural diversity and avoid what I usually call cultural erosion.

Biologists know that, when reared artificially outside their natural ecosystem, certain species can become genetically eroded if they are not fed from a healthy stock of germplasm. An example of this is *Hevea brasiliensis,* the rubber tree. Transported to Malaysia, the mother trees need to be continually fed with native seeds from the Amazon to maintain their genetic make-up. In the case of culture, a development model that is unable to preserve diversity begins to decline into a process of cultural erosion.

For me, in particular, the Report closely related to my own life experience. I have no academic expertise regarding the environment and development. I am a secondary school history teacher and, over the last 32 years, I have dedicated myself to the socio-environmental struggle in Brazil. So, my perspective is characterised by two sources of learning: that of my life as a socio-environmental militant, on my role in the field of federal parliamentary representation, my experience as a Senator for over ten years and as Minister for the Environment for over five years.

Even without that academic background, I would risk adding three other dimensions to the sustainability equation. When pondering them, I took into account the dimensions outlined in the Report, which are espoused and developed by the United Nations in protocols, conventions and international agreements. Despite often not being implemented, both globally and in nation states, its contents are absolutely valid and cannot be ignored. As such, through experience, my belief is that a development model should also include dimensions of aesthetic, political and ethical sustainability to be truly sustainable.

The dimension of aesthetic sustainability advocates that certain elements of the natural environment need to be preserved, not because of their economic potential, not because of the environmental service that they provide but because of their symbolic value, their aesthetic value, for being part of our visual memory.

A good example of what I mean is the Pão de Açúcar (Sugarloaf Mountain), the well-known landscape of the city of Rio de Janeiro, in Brazil. It could be summed up as a metamorphic rock monolith formed over 600 million years ago, but it is also a natural beauty (sculpted by the hand of God himself, for those who believe, or by the hand of nature for those who don't) that boasts aesthetic sustainability, part of the identity of a society and one of the planet's landmarks, the sight of which is an intrinsic part of our quality of life, and so should undoubtedly be preserved.

From this perspective, to be seen as sustainable, a development model would have to incorporate an intangible value of natural wealth and non-material assets. The atavistic need that the inhabitants of major cities have for contact with the elements of nature is an example of how this dimension cannot be neglected nor considered a lower priority when vying with an excessively pragmatic and narrow view of the use of natural resources.

Another of the added dimensions, that of political sustainability, is one of the most important. All of the other dimensions depend on it directly. When reading institutional reports and their set of proposals, when examining the literature produced in relation to the issue of environment and seeing the scientific and technological advances made by humanity, the general conclusion one arrives at is that, in the majority of cases, problems seem to have no solution, not because of the lack of technical expertise or unsuitable proposals, but rather because we lack ethics.

In this area, where the technical and ethical meet, politics is also present in the field of decision-making and on the scale that only the state's actions can induce. Therefore, it is fundamental that politics is sustainable so that the development process is in line with the values of sustainability.

What are the implications of sustainable politics? Primarily, it is the action of a political individual aware of their obligations, duties and rights; the action of someone who does not transfer their specific responsibility to another in relation to the collective. In addition to this, no government, no head of state, no leadership whose actions are guided by the principles of democracy will be capable of making changes without clear delegation from an informed population, capable of taking political, economic and social responsibility for such a direction.

The alteration of the development model, as expressed in the transition/mutation from its predatory form to a sustainable one, will require a civilising effort from conscious individuals, capable of giving the terms of reference for political action and demanding its attainment. This term of reference certainly includes the demand for long-term policies, although nowadays this is clearly incompatible with the short-term nature of party and electoral interests. In other words, instead of immediate policies that benefit individuals or groups on a political level, sustainability requires reconnecting politics and the socially legitimate sense of service, geared towards the real needs of the population and the interests of the country, with an awareness of the future when acting in the short term.

There needs to be an inversion of the predominant logic of current political systems, which is deeply damaging to societies and which puts the struggle for power before the concept of politics as a public forum, as a highly visible place for participation, for negotiation and for the creation of a solid social foundation for decisions of a republican nature. Instead of short-term policies to extend political careers, it is socially legitimate long-term policies that should be part of the short term of politicians.

Using the case of global warming as an example, it is obvious that, to reduce greenhouse gas emissions by 80% by 2050, major efforts need to be made in all sectors of society and there has to be engagement on the part of governments. This is certainly not achieved with a utilitarian view of politics, hence the essential need for political force on the part of society. In the case of Brazil, regardless of which party is in power, society should demand policies that combat deforestation, focus on renewable energies and encourage increases in production by improved productivity instead of the expansion of the agricultural frontier. Such policies are not a given in the state's actions, even if national legislation and protocols of intention dictate just that. Each political group that forms a government can, within the legal framework, choose and define priorities, depending on interests that may not coincide with those that the population most expects.

As such, in Brazil, whoever is in power will have to invest in science, technology, innovation in search of new products, new materials and new solutions for crises. Undoubtedly, crises are also great opportunities for new forums that create jobs and income and improve the quality of life for the population. They will also have to think about the vocational training of young people for the new areas of the creative economy, for the truly green economy and, in addition to this, they will have to create new forms of inclusion for poor families, beyond policies of income support, establishing mechanisms for productive inclusion and social emancipation.

On the other hand, political sustainability is also concerned with the role of the political player, which is one of protagonist and not spectator. When interacting with public powers, they should be highly vigilant so that investment is made according to the guidelines based on the idea of a sustainable future.

My third addition relates to the dimension of ethical sustainability, which I consider the basis of all of this. The Brundtland Report is shaped by this sense of ethical emergency, of a civilisational inflection. It deals with issues such as agriculture and the environment, cities and the environment, economic development and environment, energy generation and the environment, and points to the realisation, already presented here, that a large proportion of the problems identified are not resolved because of a lack of technical solutions but, in fact, because the technical is not yet subject to public ethics.

It is impossible to consider the integration that is an essential part of sustainability while ignoring this pressing ethical debate. The complex interactions of sectors and cultures, the collaborative attitude required and the pooling of various knowledge areas (from the traditional to the academic) depend on the oxygen that only ethics can provide, as a universal tool of effectiveness.

In short, the original and innovative dynamic inherent to sustainable development can only exist if guided by a strong value system. That is the meaning of ethical sustainability.

A dramatic example of the urgency of observing that dimension of sustainability can be seen when one looks at our legacy for future generations. The Report warns that, faced with the environmental damage done by current generations, future generations will be unable to hold them to account for today's wasteful and unsustainable lifestyle. There are a number of impediments to the effective exercise of citizenship by future generations as they do not vote, they have no financial or political power, nor can they oppose our decisions. In reality, we are trampling on their stock of rights and options without ever taking them into consideration. We are developing an unethical relationship with the future of life itself and, as a consequence, with our descendants. And all with total impunity, the greatest impunity that humanity can have.

Without the ethical dimension of sustainability, our legacy will be the decline and lack of intergenerational solidarity. What we can conclude is that the environment cannot be exploited to exhaustion, generating profit that is concentrated and accumulated as assets for a select few, but rather, it should be used to constantly aid successive generations on the planet. The only force capable of halting and reversing this selfish process is the consolidation of public ethics as a value that is a part of all plans we have for development.

After the general introduction of the idea of sustainable development, it is important to emphasise why the Report needs to be updated, not in terms of its vision, which, as I previously mentioned, remains contemporary, but rather in terms of the state of the art in each of the sectors contained therein and the general situation of the global environment.

One of the ways of updating the *Our Common Future* Report is by integrating and adjusting it to a low-carbon economy, a growing economy, but also one that does not increase the emissions of greenhouse gases, as that process is undermining the chances of maintaining and sustaining life on the planet.

Another very important aspect to update is the focus that the Report gives to the environmental impact of the poorest populations. The Report presents them as the most vulnerable, which is quite true; however, it also presents them as those who have the most impact on natural resources. If we agree that every population has an impact on the environment it lives in, it is also true that there are degrees of impact and that it can be broadly ranked. We know that the majority of the impact caused on natural bases of our development originates from those who, despite boasting higher levels of formal education and access to knowledge, create huge pressure on the planet's natural resources via their unbridled consumption, which is increasingly demanding and disposable, as well as unconcerned with the future consequences of such habits.

Here we find a paradox. Those who consume less are the ones who suffer most, as well as being portrayed as the villains of environmental impact. Those who emit less are the ones most affected by global warming and the loss of biodiversity. If we consider that the economy of developing countries depends greatly on their biodiversity, and that today we lose a thousand times more biodiversity than 50 years ago, we will have an idea of the extent of the damage imposed on those less able to deal with it. To this end, updating the Report is important to show that the pressure on natural resources comes from those with less favourable economic, social and cultural conditions, and, to a greater degree, from those who, even aware of the extent and urgency of the planetary environmental crisis, refuse to forego excessive consumption. It is worth reflecting here upon that apparently irrational social trend. Consumption occurs through necessity and also as a way of demarcating a place of power in society. Another reason is that, in addition to status, people get caught up in the intricate paths of hedonism. The creation of meanings and identities via symbols of doing, having and appearing, and not with reference to being, is part of the ideology of the consumer society.

Nowadays, we can draw certain conclusions using the elements the Report provides to analyse development on a global level. One of them is that it is difficult to consider changing the current development model based simply on questioning the way the process works. It is true that it is based on the use of fossil fuels and this is denounced and explained in great detail in the Brundtland Report. It is equally true that this development occurs at the cost of soil degradation, air pollution and the contamination of waters, springs and water tables.

Development, as we know it, is therefore a process of major losses. However, it is not enough to seek a way out of that situation solely by criticising the model that humanity has used throughout the world. First, there is a need for a more thorough questioning that focuses more on values. Here it is clear that the inappropriate way of doing comes from the inappropriate way of being. The search for more technology is useless if the basic understanding of the world remains the same, as it is pointless seeking transformations if the idea of happiness relates to the capacity for increasing consumption of material goods. According to this, well-being is clearly connected to consumption and it matters not if we forego helping others or if we are not guided by a sense of solidarity.

It is necessary to question that voraciousness that leads to the destruction of thousands and thousands of years of resources for the profit and consumption of just a few decades, obtained by a minority of the world's population. It is therefore essential to show what we are, what we have become. The questioning will necessarily focus on our way of producing and consuming and on that deep-rooted notion of happiness. It is in this way that we would arrive at the comprehensive explanation of the real causes of the set of dubious procedures that are an intrinsic part of what is called development.

The sustainable development mentioned in the Brundtland Report, which we must develop further, therefore needs to be seen as a way of being, not only as a way of doing; not as an adaptation of what we have so that it has slightly less impact, but as a complete concept that is capable of giving the appropriate support to an ideal of a future; like a kind of motor that will not be on the prow by way of ideological decoration, a source of self-satisfaction and ostentation, but rather at the stern, as the Brazilian psychoanalyst Fabio Hermann said,[237] to help us set off and lead us to new levels of civilisation, where human beings can establish a relationship of respect with themselves, with other human beings and with nature. It is because we have the capacity to put into words what we do in relation to nature that we have the responsibility, based on our actions, to redefine the meaning of that relationship.

Sustainability requires from us a type of creative de-adaptation, a concept that originates from Argentinean psychoanalyst Jorge Gonçalves da Cruz,[238] who exemplifies it with our choice of profession. Often, that choice causes great disillusionment over the course of one's life. Instead of adapting ourselves to it and continuing to be unhappy, he says we should creatively de-adapt to re-signify that experience and change to something that can give us greater satisfaction and which is more productive.

Transplanting that idea of creative de-adaptation to the level of society, it is possible to realise that, rather than an adaptation to error, we have the opportunity for a creative de-adaptation from the way we undertake our economic, social and cultural development and which many consider a fate we are powerless to change. And yet, until very recently, responding to the question of how energy is produced, knowledge from the 20th century would answer: using mainly coal, oil and gas. And this would not be merely an issue of a technological stage or the choice of non-sustainable technologies.

The Brazilian psycho-pedagogue Nadia Bossa says that reality responds in the same language in which it is questioned.[239] I therefore conclude that reality is a polyglot. It is us who are monolingual. *Our Common Future* is a denouncement of that poverty in terms of language, the word, in the relationship with nature. The economic crisis the world is enduring is also a condemnation of all of this. Asking the question in a different way, assuming that reality is a polyglot and we are monoglots, it would be possible to enrich our language, learning from reality.

Certain people are capable of doing so; they have an anticipatory view of the world dynamic and think ahead, they think of alternatives. Via these people, in relation to the question on ways of obtaining energy, it would be possible to respond that, in the 21st century, within the context of the global crisis shaped by the Armageddon of climate change, energy can be produced from biomass, wind, sun, water and many other sources. The Italian psychoanalyst Mário Alletti observes,[240] in a way that is very appropriate to the reasoning developed here, that humanity made use of the force of the winds to sail before scientists discovered the laws of wind dynamics.

Sustainable development cannot be seen as something that has to be finished and ready in order to be useful, to be applied. Often, anxiety underestimates complexity and wants straightforward answers (or 'concrete' answers); it does not take into consideration that no one, no country or society knows of or is using a finished model. Our social and economic processes are appropriations adapted from a set of influences and concepts that are as contemporary as they are historic. The most important thing is that there are people capable of using the force of the wind before discovering the laws of wind dynamics. There are people who are creating sustainability when they do research on energy production using the wind, the sun and so many other renewable and safe sources to achieve another development model. This means setting off on the path before having all the answers. And so, sustainability is related to this creative de-adaptation, a productive de-continuity, according to the previously cited Jorge Cruz.[241]

What is a productive discontinuity? It is a situation where the solution for a problem is not exactly known, but continuing in the same vein is not an option. Continuing in the same direction will be the equivalent of going over the edge and falling into the abyss; sometimes the way out is simply stopping. Sometimes, it means trying alternatives. And it is these alternatives that are the main indicators of the path ahead in the present. *Our Common Future*, now nearly 25 years old, boasts the merit of pushing humanity in that prospective, challenging, de-adapting direction.

Sustainable development, seen not as simply a way of doing things but emphatically as a way of being, from the perspective of creative adaptation, should seek a basis of sustenance. And what is that basis? It could be something very simple, like a kind of reconnection with civilisation in its infancy. Until very recently, humanity advanced guided by the ideal of being. The Romans wanted to be great and strong. The Greeks wanted to be wise and free. In the Middle Ages, the ideal was that of sanctity, despite the many sins that were committed in its name.

From this came mercantilism, and being an artisan became making artefacts. Being a scientist and being a philosopher became creating science. Being a saint became creating tithes, followers, churches. And to cut a long story short, and bring us back to the 21st century, even an amorous relationship between two people became making love. In a culture that sets doing, doing, doing, above all other things, one becomes suffocated by the products generated by that ethos. This is where we are. We no longer know how to live without things. Everything is there. The difference is that many people cannot have access to everything that exists, and so they become excluded from the codes of social classification that base themselves on the capacity to consume everything that the material cultural produces.

Although they are aware of environmental problems, young people are trained, taught and encouraged to always consume more and are transformed by the deification of consumption into veritable destroyers of the future, however unwittingly, even if that is not their aim in life. Indeed, it is not new data that shows us that if the consumption patterns of the populations of rich countries were emulated by all 7 billion human beings on the planet, we would need five planet Earths. However, we only have one, which means that its material and cultural bases cannot be made universal. And, so, those bases cannot be defended, in terms of ethics and justice, unless we want to institutionalise the existence of people naturally destined to live well and other to live poorly: in other words, first-class and second-class people.

Here, there is a dilemma because what makes us humanity is exactly the common sense of belonging to the human race, with rights deriving from that condition, greater than any differences. In fact, that was also a mistake made by so-called socialist economies that pointlessly attempted to standardise differences, suffocating individual identity. It needs to be clarified that a process based on sustainability cannot involve the dilution of aspirations or the elimination of differences. There is a civilising reflection that the Report invites us to undertake.

A good start for that effort of reflection, once again, taking on board Jorge Cruz's contribution, is that you do not ask children what they are going to do when they grow up; you ask them what they are going to be. Similarly, we need to say to ourselves, not what we want to do, but what we want to be in our relationship with nature, between each other and with other forms of existence.

Sustainability and sustainable development will not be achieved by the omnipotence of our thinking. That is a historically determined category that will have to be constructed from tangible and intangible means in an effort the shape of which we have yet to fathom; however, we are going in that direction. For sustainable development to take place, before being an answer, it has to have meaning. And its meaning should be associated with a vision, a process and new structures.

The vision that guides sustainable development needs to be generous, inclusive, widespread and with the capacity to share the leading role, achievement and recognition of this grandiose deed. There is nothing quite like meeting a challenge of this magnitude, orienting our vision via the categories we have worked with until now, especially us, those who are from the leftist tradition. Our tools for thought and action have been the concepts that express logical oppositions, impoverished by historic social experiences, like the labels of left, right and centre; hot and cold; good and bad; etc. Today, we are experiencing the challenge of paradox, if we look back at our civilisation. To deal with that question, there needs to be an inclusive effort, the first step to turning occasional alliances into ethical principles and lasting values. Those alliances do not mean homogenisation of political nuances, or the elimination of localised differences; they mean moving forward together for important causes, preserving identities. This is valid for parties, companies, academia, communities, and making possible what French sociologist Edgar Morin calls the dialogue on knowledge.[242] Answers cannot be found based only on denotative premises of right and wrong, originating from the paradigms of Western science.

For this reflection, it is important to establish that narrative knowledge has an important contribution to make. Although not a science, it is a form of knowledge because it intuitively developed methodologies of perception and listening that allowed the accumulation of precious observations and conclusions for the dialogue of knowledge. However, its contribution will sadly be lost if it comes up against the barrier of discrimination, disrespect and the ranking of knowledge.

In relation to the dialogue on knowledge, Brazil is a country that still has around 220 peoples that speak 180 different languages. The widespread assumption is that only Portuguese is spoken in Brazil; however, we are a country bursting with cultural diversity and a wealth of traditional knowledge.

It is fundamental that the process of knowledge exchange is democratic and visible. With modern means of communication, it is possible to highlight what is done within companies and governments. What is in everyone's interests cannot become a closely guarded secret of the few. This care is necessary because, as we have seen happen with intolerable regularity, we can be surprised by the revelation of what was done in secret having disastrous results and all of those who did not participate in the collusion are tragically made to foot the bill for those errors and held responsible for the damage and suffering resulting from the arrogance of the mistake. There is no need to cite examples, as what is happening now, in terms of the world economy, is common knowledge.

Another beneficial effect of a democratic process is avoiding the possibility of a supposedly generous and inclusive vision diluting differences, ignoring conflict and involving people in an oppressive equality. The inclusion is only real if it is able to produce individuals who possess the ability to ask questions and look for answers for the problems that arise in a creative, productive and free manner—this being the outcome of the meeting of individuals with different wants and different contributions.

It is also necessary to invest in a new type of leadership. It is no longer about leading with words or charisma. It is necessary to lead by what one does, by what one practises: in other words, leading by example. That is the capacity that is suited to democratic processes. There will have to be many of these new leaderships because if the problems are widespread, then leaderships need to be distributed in the same way, in addition to having the same multi-centred character. There can be no focus on definitive leaderships, anointed for all matters. Nobody can be the leader of everything. Nobody can be the leader of everything and still be the leader of the rest. The leader that the future requires will be led in areas they do not master, because legitimacy will be fundamental. I learnt this observing a very interesting movement of the artefact still used by Brazilian Indians: the bow and arrow. There are moments where a person is in the position of the bow that pushes the arrow. In other moments, those same people or institutions will be in the position of the arrow. There is a constant swapping of those positions, and so there is no fixed position within rigid structures, which cannot redesign their functional nature according to the opportunities that occur and the requirements of the processes. This would go against the nimbleness and versatility that are desirable characteristics for a vision and process based on sustainability. As such, that capacity to alternate and change functions in complex and dense processes will be features of the new leaderships, the leaderships for sustainable development, the leaderships of the 21st century.

The structures need plasticity and flexibility, which are important for academia, the arts, business, governments, spirituality and all of society's dynamic nuclei to make contributions to their technical assets and the repertoire of solutions. It is not easy to have flexible structures because we are culturally adapted to having rigid ones, so rigid that they break. Undoubtedly, those structures that intend to demonstrate power were built in this way due to a fear of showing weakness, and also because they are products of a collision culture and extreme competitiveness. However, the truth is that flexibility is not synonymous with weakness. On the contrary, it is another form of power, but a power created by the combination of forces, by the integration of contributions and diversities that can be found in the social and cultural dynamic, without any one of them being diluted, losing their identity or dominating excessively.

The Report was always an inspiration to me. When I was the Brazilian Minister for the Environment, it was a crucial reference for the implementation of very important agreements in the area of biodiversity. Taking on that position in a mega-diverse country that boasts natural heritage made up of seven very rich biomes would have weighed more heavily were it not for the support of the accumulation of knowledge and experiences of the global community as a result of the publication of *Our Common Future* in the 1980s.

That inspiration is inseparable from the results obtained by the team I led at the Ministry of the Environment. We created 24 million hectares of Conservation Units and pushed what was a rising curve of deforestation in the Amazon downwards, in a reduction that reached 80%, if we consolidate the drop of the annual deforestation rates of the last eight years.

Our legislation, which is considered to be one of the most advanced in the world, owes a debt to the contributions of *Our*

Common Future, which had a very important impact on the drawing up of the Brazilian Constitution of 1988. It was also at the root of the progress made in dealing with problems of biodiversity loss, which culminated in the creation of the Chico Mendes Biodiversity Conservation Institute to better preserve the country's nature Conservation Units. At the same time, an institution was created to devise and implement measures for the sustainable use of our forests, the Brazilian Forest Service (Serviço Brasileiro de Florestas).

In fact, the Brundtland Report inspired the environmental legislation of many countries. It helped create global governance, local governance, governance within the scope of nation states. Similarly, it was a tool to inspire businesses and governments to commit to the future that needs to be built. In line with the name it was given by the World Commission on Environment and Development, it is truly the basic document for us to build a common future. However, it is only possible to talk about a common future if we also admit that we have a common past, and a past that cannot be a ghost that binds humanity to historical errors in relation to economic, social, cultural and environmental choices. That common past needs to be recognised as the past, in order to give priority to the advent of the future.

Edgar Morin says that 'change, at the outset, is just a shift'[243] and he recommends that we be aware in order to understand which shift is the one we want to prosper. In this sense, it is clear that we cannot allow the use of fossil fuels to continue to prosper, as their carbon gas emissions may cause an increase in the world's average temperature of 4 degrees, according to scientists' recent estimates, and destroy life on the planet as a result. We cannot allow the shift that destroys the prospects of the millions of young people all over the world who are involved in the daily fight for the right to a decent future. Daniel Cohn-Bendit has repeated in speeches given all round the world that the protest movements of young people are a predictable reaction to the fact that they are being denied the opportunities to create a future in accordance with their dreams. It is still a timid response to a situation created by the choices that humanity has made to address economic, social and environmental issues over recent centuries.

This is how we are going to make the new paths of sustainability prosper, re-signifying our experience, not as a way of doing, but as a way of being; the sustainable being; the being that is reconnected to civilisation in its infancy, but now without making the mistake of fighting for any type of grandiosity but rather for everyone's quality of life and in defence of the planet.

We are enduring a serious economic crisis at the beginning of the second decade of the 21st century, but that crisis, which is widespread, cannot be the reason for us to neglect the challenge of sustainability. It is another mistake to rank the crises we are going through. Although the greater pressure and political weight of the global financial system are able to impose a favourable narrative for its problems, the social crisis, with its 2 billion starving people with no prospects of improvement, also has a frightening aspect.

However, more than the drama of these two crises, the possibility of global warming that leads to the extinction of life on the planet overshadows all other concerns. There will be no financial engineering to salvage; there will be no starving people to help if we do not take the task of considering and creating new directions for our civilisations seriously—directions that are consistent with humanity's trajectory until today, as I have tried to demonstrate in this chapter. New strategies, agreements and global institutions are needed to complete this task in the time that, I hope, still allows us to take decisions without totally losing control of our own destinies; without being swept away to a tragic end.

Sustainability is not a panacea and cannot be a concept that produces hollow consensus, of the type that generates agreements that no one abides by. Sustainability should be made up of efforts that improve the quality of economic, political, social and cultural development, on new bases of sustenance.

Alongside the tradition of global competition, there needs to be an even stronger tradition of global cooperation. Given that, until today, institutional responses have been unsuitable and insufficient for the challenge of sustainable development, it seems appropriate to consider the possibility of a global institution, in the same way that trade is represented by the World Trade Organization. This would be the first step to establishing a modern institutional body, with the right expertise, financial capacity and authority to act with the urgency required by the environmental situation, which is becoming increasingly dramatic every time that, under the pretext of a lack of resources, the opportunity to study the future of the planet with intelligence, courage and responsibility is postponed.

Notes

Introduction

1 I. Calvino, *Why Read the Classics?* (trans. M. McLaughlin; London: Jonathan Cape, 1999).

2 Ibid.

3 Ibid.

4 Ibid.

5 Ibid.

6 Ibid.

1. *Walden*

7 P.J. Crutzen and E.F. Stoermer, 'The "Anthropocene" ', *Global Change Newsletter* 41 (2000): 17-18.

8 I believe that the poem 'I hear America singing' may be considered as Whitman's motto: Walt Whitman, *Selected Poems* (New York: Avenel, Gramercy Books, 1992): 177.

9 Among the extensive secondary literature on *Walden*, I would recommend two subtle essays dealing with the architectonic complexity of Thoreau's masterpiece: R.J. Schneider, 'Walden', in J. Myerson (ed.), *The Cambridge Companion to Henry David Thoreau* (Cambridge: Cambridge University Press, 1995): 92-106; H. Daniel Peck, 'Thoreaus's Lake

of Light: Modes of Representation and the Enactment of Philosophy in Walden', *Midwest Studies in Philosophy* 28 (2004): 85-101.

10 Henry David Thoreau, *Walden and Civil Disobedience* (New York: Penguin Books, 1986): 135.

11 Viriato Soromenho-Marques, 'Sinopse histórico-biográfica', Dissertação *sobre o Governo*, de John C. Calhoun (Lisboa: Círculo de Leitores/ Temas & Debates, 2010): 67-71.

12 *Walden*: 240.

13 The concept of the 'two cultures' divide was cited in C.P. Snow's famous 1959 lecture; however, it mirrored a much older scientific and philosophical debate. Charles Percy Snow, *The Two Cultures* (with an Introduction by S. Collini; Cambridge: Cambridge University Press, 2003).

14 R.W. Emerson, *Nature and Other Writings* (ed. P. Turner; Boston; London: Shambhala, 1994): 382.

15 *Walden*: 50.

16 Ibid.: 47.

17 Ibid.: 77.

18 'Wie viel Wahrheit erträgt, wie viel Wahrheit wagt ein Geist? Das wurde für mich immer mehr der eigentliche Werthmesser.' Nietzsche, *Ecce Homo*, *Sämmtliche Werke* (ed. G. Colli and M. Montinari; Berlin, De Gruyter, 1980), 6: 259.

19 *Walden*: 57. Emerson was among the preferred readings of Nietzsche. He considered Emerson as a 'twin-soul' (*Bruder-Seele*): Nietzsche, letter to Franz Overbeck, 14 December 1883, *Sämmtliche Briefe* (ed. G. Colli and M. Montinari; Berlin: De Gruyter, 1986) 6: 463.

20 *Walden*: 48. Marx developed the concept of 'alienated work' (*entfremdete Arbeit*) in his 1844 manuscript *Ökonomisch-philosophische Manuskripte*.

21 *Walden*: 136.

22 Ibid.: 112-14.

23 Ibid.: 180-1.

24 Ibid.: 240.

25 'Nature may be selfishly studied as trade. Astronomy to the selfish becomes astrology' (Emerson, *Nature and Other Writings*: 387-8). Emerson also denounces in a rather surprising way the artificial barriers between mind and nature, showing that all beings are different modes of thought: 'Nature is the incarnation of a thought, and turns to a thought, again, as ice becomes water and gas. The world is mind precipitated, and the volatile essence is forever escaping again into the state of free thought. Hence the virtue and pungency of the influence on

the mind of natural objects, whether inorganic or organic. Man imprisoned, man crystallized, man vegetative, speaks to man impersonated'
(Emerson, *Nature and Other Writings*: 400-401).

26 *Walden*: 114.

27 Thoreau, *Civil Disobedience*: 389.

28 Ibid.: 395.

29 'I say, break the law. Let your life be a counter friction to stop the
machine … I think that it is enough if they have God on their side,
without waiting for that other one. Moreover, any man more right than
his neighbors constitutes a majority of one already' (Ibid.: 396-7).

30 Ibid.: 413.

31 If we go beyond *Walden*, we have to remember how *Civil Disobedience* was key to the political gesture and methods that drove Mahatma
Gandhi in achieving independence for India.

32 In 1956, Rachel Carson published an essay dedicated to her nephew,
Roger, in the *Woman's Home Companion* magazine, entitled 'Help Your
Child to Wonder'. Recently this essay was published with photos: R.
Carson and N. Kelsh, *The Sense of Wonder* (New York: HarperCollins,
1998). The link between a reverence for nature and moral improvement, a key element in Thoreau's stance, is clearly also found in Carson's pedagogical approaches to natural beauties and landscapes.

33 'It is scarcely necessary to remark that a stationary condition implies
no stationary state of human improvement. There would be all kinds
of mental culture, and moral and social progress; [and] much room
for improving the Art of Living' (John Stuart Mill [1848], *Principles of
Political Economy with Some of Their Applications to Social Philosophy* [New York: Reprints of Economic Classics, Augustus M. Kelley,
1965]: 746).

34 'If you have built castles in the air, your work need not to be lost; that is
where they should be. Now put the foundations under them' (*Walden*:
372).

2. A Sand County Almanac

35 See C. Meine, *Aldo Leopold: His Life and Work* (Madison: University of
Wisconsin Press, 1988, 2010).

36 See, for example, 'To the Forest Officers of the Carson' (1913) in S.L.
Flader and J.B. Callicott (eds), *The River of the Mother of God and
Other Essays by Aldo Leopold* (Madison: University of Wisconsin
Press, 1991): 41-6.

37 See, for example, 'The Conservation Ethic' (1930) in Flader and Callicott, *The River of the Mother of God*: 81-208.

38 Meine, *Aldo Leopold*.

39 Ibid.

40 D. Ribbens, 'The Making of *A Sand County Almanac*', in J. Baird Callicott (ed.), *Companion to* A Sand County Almanac: *Interpretive and Critical Essays* (Madison: University of Wisconsin Press, 1987): 92-3.

41 Ibid.: 99.

42 Ibid.: 93.

43 Meine, *Aldo Leopold*.

44 Both Meine, *Aldo Leopold*, and Ribbens, 'The Making', provide accounts of the posthumous publication process.

45 A. Leopold, *A Sand County Almanac and Sketches Here and There* (New York: Oxford University Press, 1949): viii.

46 Ribbens, 'The Making': 102.

47 Ibid.: 102.

48 Leopold, *Sand County*: viii.

49 J. Tallmadge, 'Anatomy of a Classic', in Callicott (ed.), *Companion*: 110-27.

50 Leopold, *Sand County*: viii.

51 Ibid.: 204-205.

52 Lynn White Jr, 'The Historical Roots of our Ecologic Crisis', *Science* 155 (1967): 1203-1207.

53 Leopold, *Sand County*: ix.

54 Ibid.: viii.

55 Henry David Thoreau, *Walden or Life in the Woods* (Boston: Ticknor & Fields, 1854).

56 Leopold, *Sand County*: viii-ix.

57 Ibid.: ix.

58 Ibid., emphasis added.

59 Ibid.: 3, emphasis added.

60 Ibid.: 4, emphasis added.

61 Ibid.

62 Ibid.

63 C. Elton, *Animal Ecology* (London: Sidgwick & Jackson, 1927).

64 Leopold, *Sand County*: 18, emphasis added.

65 Ibid.

66 Ibid.: 18-19.

67 Ibid.: 19, emphasis added.

68 Ibid.: 20, emphasis added.

69 Ibid., emphasis added.

70 Ibid.

71 Ibid.: 20-1.

72 Ibid.: 95.

73 Ibid.: 96.

74 Ibid.

75 P. Fritzell, 'The Conflicts of Ecological Conscience', in Callicott (ed.), *Companion*: 147.

76 M. Arnold, 'From the Hymn of Empedocles', in Arthur Quiller-Couch (ed.), *Oxford Book of English Verse, 1250–1900* (Oxford: Clarendon Press, 1919): #754.

77 This sentence was deleted from the four-part expanded (and apparently bowdlerised!) version of the book published by Ballantine as *A Sand County Almanac and Essays on Conservation from Round River* in 1966.

78 Leopold, *Sand County*: 66.

79 Ibid.: 108.

80 Ibid.

81 Ibid.: 107-108.

82 A. Tansley, 'The Use and Abuse of Vegetational Concepts and Terms', *Ecology* 16 (1935): 284-307.

83 Ibid.: 299.

84 Leopold, *Sand County*: 215.

85 D. Worster, *Nature's Economy: A History of Ecological Ideas* (San Francisco: Sierra Club Books, 1977).

86 R. Lindeman, 'The Trophic-Dynamic Aspect of Ecology', *Ecology* 23 (1942): 399-418.

87 Leopold, *Sand County*: 216, emphasis added.

88 Ibid.: 149.

89 Ibid.

90 Ibid., emphasis added.

91 Ibid.: 130.

92 Ibid.

93 Ibid.

94 Ibid.: 130-2.

95 For the date and place of the event, see Meine, *Aldo Leopold*.

96 Ribbens, 'The Making': 96.

97 Ibid.

98 Acts 22:7.

99   Leopold, *Sand County*: 173-4. Babbitt is the title character—a militantly ignorant real estate salesman, booster and social climber—of a novel by Sinclair Lewis, satirising the prevailing middle-class American beliefs, attitudes and values of the 1920s.

100 See A.J. Ayer, *Language, Truth, and Logic* (London: Victor Gollancz, 1936).

101 M. Black, 'The Gap Between "Is" and "Should" ', *Philosophical Review* 73 (1964): 165-81.

102 A. Leopold, 'The Conservation Ethic', *Journal of Forestry* 31 (1933): 634-43, emphasis added.

103 I. Kant, *Grounding for the Metaphysics of Morals* (trans. J.W. Ellington; Indianapolis, IN: Hackett, 1993): 40.

104 Leopold, *Sand County*: 223.

105 Charles Darwin, *The Descent of Man and Selection in Relation to Sex* (London: John Murray, 2nd edn, 1874).

106 Leopold, *Sand County*: 203-204, emphasis added.

107 Darwin, *Descent*: 126-7.

108 Leopold, *Sand County*: 204.

109 Ibid.

110 Ibid.: 224-5.

111 W. Vogt, *Road to Survival* (New York: William Sloan Associates, 1948).

112 R. Bass, 'Introduction by Rick Bass', in R. Bedichek, *Adventures with a Texas Naturalist* (Austin: University of Texas Press, 1947/1994): v-xvii.

113 Tallmadge, 'Anatomy': 115.

114 Ibid.: 116.

115 Ibid.: 115.

116 Ibid.: 116.

117 Ibid.

118 Ibid.: 119.

119 Ibid.: 123.

120 Meine, *Aldo Leopold*.

121 A. Leopold, 'The Forestry of the Prophets', *Journal of Forestry* 18 (1920): 412-19: 412.

122 A. Leopold, 'Some Fundamentals of Conservation in the Southwest', *Environmental Ethics* 1 (1979): 131-41: 139.

123 Tallmadge, 'Anatomy': 116.

124 Acts 17:28.

125 See W. Stegner, 'The Legacy of Aldo Leopold', in Callicott (ed.), *Companion*: 233-45, for both the Bible and prophet tropes; see R. Mann,

'Aldo Leopold: Priest and Prophet', *American Forests* 60.8 (August 1954): 23, 42-3, for an early use of the prophet trope; see E. Swift, 'Aldo Leopold: Wisconsin's Conservation Prophet', *Wisconsin Tales and Trails* 2.2 (September 1961): 2-5, for a continuation of the prophet trope; see R. Nash, 'Aldo Leopold: Prophet', in *Wilderness and the American Mind* (New Haven, CT: Yale University Press, 1967): 182-99, for a popularising of the prophet trope and burning it into the collective consciousness of American environmentalism.

126 Elton, *Animal Ecology*.

127 J.T. Curtis, *The Vegetation of Wisconsin* (Madison: University of Wisconsin Press, 1959); R.P. McIntosh, 'The Continuum Concept of Vegetation', *Botanical Review* (1967) 33: 130-87; R.H. Whittaker, 'A Criticism of the Plant Association and Climatic Climax Concepts', *Northwest Science* 25 (1951): 18-31.

128 Tansley, 'Use and Abuse': 300, emphasis added.

129 A. Leopold, 'The Arboretum and the University', *Parks and Recreation* 18.2 (1934): 59-60: 59.

130 F. Clements, *Research Methods in Ecology* (Lincoln, NB: University Publishing Company, 1905); F.E. Clements, *Plant Succession: The Analysis of the Development of Vegetation* (Washington: Carnegie Institution; Publication no. 242, 1916).

131 See especially D. Worster, *Nature's Economy: A History of Ecological Ideas* (Cambridge: Cambridge University Press, 1977).

132 Tansley, 'Use and Abuse': 289, 291, 300.

133 E.P. Odum, 'The Strategy of Ecosystem Development', *Science* 164 (1969): 260-70.

134 Elton, *Animal Ecology*; A. Leopold, 'A Biotic View of Land', *Journal of Forestry* 37 (1939): 727-30; Leopold, *Sand County*; R.L. Lindeman, 'Trophic-Dynamic Aspect'; Tansley, 'Use and Abuse'.

135 Leopold, *Sand County*: 221.

136 Ibid.: 223.

137 Ibid.: 214.

138 R.V. O'Neill, D.L. DeAngelis, J.B. Waide and T.F.H. Allen, *A Hierarchical Concept of Ecosystems* (Princeton, NJ: Princeton University Press, 1986).

139 T.F.H. Allen and T.W. Hoekstra, *Toward a Unified Ecology* (New York: Columbia University Press, 1992).

140 H.A. Gleason, 'The Individualistic Concept of the Plant Association', *Bulletin of the Torrey Botanical Club* 53 (1926): 1-20; R.H. Whittaker, 'Gradient Analysis of Vegetation', *Biological Review* 28 (1967): 207-64;

R.P. McIntosh, 'H.A. Gleason, "Individualistic Ecologist", 1882–1975', *Bulletin of the Torrey Botanical Club* 102 (1975): 253-73.

141   S.T.A. Pickett and P.S. White, *The Ecology of Natural Disturbance and Patch Dynamics* (Orlando, FL: Academic Press, 1995).

142   S.T.A. Pickett and R.S. Ostfeld, 'The Shifting Paradigm in Ecology', in R.L. Knight and S.F. Bates (eds), *A New Century for Natural Resources Management* (Washington: Island Press, 1995): 261-78.

143   I. Douglas, D. Goode, M. Houk and R. Wang, *The Routledge Handbook of Urban Ecology* (New York: Routledge, 2011).

144   J. Baird Callicott, *Beyond the Land Ethic: More Essays in Environmental Philosophy* (Albany: State University of New York Press, 1999).

145   White, 'Historical Roots'; I. McHarg, *Design with Nature* (New York: Natural History Press, 1969); R. Dawkins, *The God Delusion* (London: Bantam Press, 2006); B. Maher, *Religulous*—a film documentary, 2008.

146   T. Berry, *The Sacred Universe: Earth, Spirituality and Religion in the 21st Century* (ed. Mary Evelyn Tucker; New York: Columbia University Press, 2009); B. Swimme and T. Berry, *The Universe Story: From the Primordial Flaring Forth to the Ecozoic Era—A Celebration of the Unfolding of the Cosmos* (New York: HarperCollins, 1992).

147   I thank Curt Meine, Leopold's biographer, and Buddy Huffaker, Director of the Aldo Leopold Foundation, for reading an earlier version of this essay and providing me with corrective critical comments.

3. Rachel Carson's *Silent Spring*

148   L. Lear, 'Introduction', in *Silent Spring* (New York: Mariner Books, Houghton Mifflin, 40th anniversary edn, 2002): xi.

149   Ibid.: xiv.

150   'Acknowledgments' in *Silent Spring*. All quotations from *Silent Spring* refer to the 40th Anniversary Edition (2002) published by Mariner Books, Houghton Mifflin Co.

151   Lear, 'Introduction', x-xi.

152   P.M. Vitousek, H.A. Mooney, J. Lubchenco and J.M. Melillo, 'Human Domination of Earth's Ecosystems', *Science* 277 (1997): 494-99.

153   S.J. Scherr and J.A. McNeely, 'Biodiversity Conservation and Agricultural Sustainability: Towards a New Paradigm of "Ecoagriculture" Landscapes', in *Philosophical Transactions of the Royal Society* (review issue on sustainable agriculture) (10 July 2006).

154   Carson, *Silent Spring*: 293.

155   Ibid.: 293.

156 Ibid.: 296.
157 Ibid.: 296.
158 Ibid.: 296.
159 Ibid.: 296-7.
160 Ibid.: 246.
161 Ibid.: 132.
162 Ibid.: 246.
163 Ibid.: 188.
164 Ibid.: 12.
165 Ibid.: 12-13.
166 Ibid.: 277-8.
167 J. Kloppenburg, 'Social Theory and the De/Reconstruction of Agricultural Science: Local Knowledge for an Alternative Agriculture', *Rural Sociology* 56.4 (1991): 519-48.
168 Carson, *Silent Spring*: 149.
169 Ibid.: 258-9.
170 Ibid.: 259.
171 G. Vanloqueren and P.V. Baret, 'How Agricultural Research Systems Shape a Technological Regime that Develops Genetic Engineering but Locks out Agroecological Innovations', *Research Policy* 38 (2009): 971-83.
172 Carson, *Silent Spring*: 258-9.

4. *The Limits to Growth* revisited

173 D.H. Meadows, D.L. Meadows, J. Randers and W.W. Behrens III, *The Limits to Growth: A Report for the Club of Rome's Project on the Predicament of Mankind* (New York: Universe Books, 1972).
174 Club of Rome, *Annual Report* (Vienna: Club of Rome, 2004).
175 See T. O'Riordan (ed.), *Environmental Science for Environmental Management* (New York: Harlow: Prentice Hall, 2000): 40.
176 P. Ehrlich and A. Ehrlich, *The Population Bomb* (New York: Sierra Club/Ballantine Books, 1968). For an update see the July 2011 issue of the *Electronic Journal of Sustainable Development* (www.ejsd.org).
177 E. Pestel and M. Mesarovic, *Mankind at the Turning Point* (New York: HarperCollins, 1974).
178 D. Meadows, D. Meadows and J. Randers, *Beyond the Limits: Global Collapse or Sustainable Future* (London: Earthscan, 1993); D.H. Meadows, J. Randers and D.L. Meadows, *Limits to Growth: The 30-Year Update* (White River Junction, VT: Chelsea Green, 2004); D. Meadows,

'Limits to Growth Revisited: Forty Years On', Lecture, Brussels, November 2011.

179 G. Turner, 'A Comparison of *The Limits to Growth* with Thirty Years of Reality', *Global Environmental Change* 18 (2008): 398-411: 401.

180 www.clubofrome.org/?p=324.

181 For a comprehensive history of the origins of *Limits* and the early reactions, see R. McCutcheon, *Limits of a Modern World: A Study of the Limits to Growth Debate* (London: Butterworth, 1979).

182 Meadows *et al., Beyond the Limits*: 234.

183 Ibid.: 225.

184 A. Peccei, *One Hundred Pages for Society* (New York: Pergamon Press, 1981): 184-5.

185 Turner, 'A Comparison': 396.

186 J. Simon, *The Ultimate Resource* (Princeton, NJ: Princeton University Press, 1981).

187 E. von Weizsäcker, A.B. Lovins and L.H. Lovins, *Factor Four: Doubling Wealth; Halving Resource Use* (London: Earthscan, 1998).

188 Turner, 'A Comparison': 401.

189 Simon, *The Ultimate Resource*: 41.

190 G.O. Barney, *Global 2000 Report to the President: Entering the Twenty-First Century* (Washington, DC: Council on Environmental Quality and the US Department of State, 1980–1981).

191 J. Simon and H. Kahn (eds), *The Resourceful Earth: A Response to the Global 2000 Report* (New York: Basil Blackwell, 1984): 45.

192 P.D. Aligica, 'Julian Simon and the Limits to Growth Malthusianism', *Electronic Journal of Sustainable Development* 1.3 (2011): 8-16.

193 Meadows *et al., Beyond the Limits*.

194 Meadows *et al., The 30-Year Update*.

195 J. Stiglitz, A. Sen and J.-P. Fitoussi, *Report by the Commission on the Measurement of Economic Performance and Social Progress* (Paris: International Commission on the Measurement of Economic Performance and Social Progress, 2008).

196 R. Layard, *Happiness: Lessons from a New Science* (Harmondsworth, UK: Penguin, 2011).

197 T. Jackson, *Prosperity without Growth: Economics for a Finite Planet* (London: Earthscan, 2011).

198 *Resurgence,* 'Wellbeing: Happy People, Happy Planet', *Resurgence* 269 (November/December 2011): 8-44.

199 Turner, 'A Comparison'.

200 Ibid.: 408-9.

201 M. Lynas, *The God Species: How the Planet Can Survive the Age of Humans* (London: Fourth Estate Press, 2011).

202 See T. O'Riordan, J. Cameron and A. Jordan (eds.), *Reinterpreting the Precautionary Principle* (London: Cameron & May, 2000).

203 For the best exposition see M. Hulme, *Why We Disagree about Climate Change: Understanding, Controversy, Inaction, and Opportunity* (London: Earthscan, 2010): 92-108.

204 IEA, 'Executive summary', *World Energy Outlook* (Paris: International Energy Agency, 2011): 1.

205 R.L. Moss, E. Tzimas, H. Kara, P. Willis and J. Kooroshy, *Critical Metals in Strategic Energy Technologies* (Petten, Netherlands: Joint Research Centre, Institute for Energy and Transport, 2011).

206 EWEA, 'Rare earths: wind power NOT a major user', press release, 28 October 2011 (www.ewea.org/index.php?id=60&no_cache=1&tx_ttnews%5Btt_news%5D=1917&tx_ttnews%5BbackPid%5D=259&cHash=086c14fdb3103002e307de5ff488ddc9).

207 *New Scientist*, 2 April 2011: 8-9.

208 Ibid.: 11.

209 roadmap2050.eu/downloads.

210 Intergovernmental Panel on Climate Change, *Special Report on Renewable Energy* (Bonn: IPCC, 2011): 7-8.

211 F. Hirsch, *Social Limits to Growth* (New York: Basic Books, 1991).

212 *Resurgence,* 'Wellbeing'.

213 J. Rockström, W. Steffen, K. Noone, Å. Persson *et al.*, 'Planetary Boundaries: Exploring the Safe Operating Space for Humanity', *Ecology and Society* 14.2 (2009): 32 and *Nature* 461 (24 September 2009): 472-5.

214 K. Raworth, *Planetary Boundaries and Social Boundaries: Defining a Safe and Just Operating Space for Humanity* (Godalming: WWF-UK, 2011).

215 www.guardian.co.uk/environment/2011/oct/11/osborne-treasury-attacked-green-policies.

216 See P. Kumar, *The Economics of Ecosystems and Biodiversity: Ecologic and Economic Foundations* (London: Earthscan, 2010).

217 Meadows *et al.*, *Beyond the Limits*: 24.

218 Ibid.: 224-36.

219 See S. Parkin, *The Positive Deviant: Leadership in a Perverse World* (London: Earthscan, 2010).

5. Small is still beautiful

220 E.F. Schumacher, *Small is Beautiful: Economics as if People Matter* (London: Vintage Books, 1993): 49. This edition is the source of all the Schumacher extracts in this chapter.

221 Ibid.: 51.

222 Ibid.: 169.

223 Ibid.: 202.

224 Ibid.: 203.

225 Ibid.: 204.

226 Ibid.: 5.

227 Ibid.: 8.

228 Ibid.: 20.

229 Ibid.: 20.

230 Ibid.: 20.

231 Ibid.: 31.

232 Ibid.: 41.

233 Ibid.: 43.

234 Ibid.: 43.

235 Ibid.: 96.

236 Barbara Wood, *Alias Papa: A Life of Fritz Schumacher* (Oxford University Press, 1985): 248.

6. An essay on *Our Common Future*

237 Fabio Hermann, *O que é Psicanálise* (Coleção Primeiros Passos; Brazil: Editora Brasiliense): 10.

238 Personal communication with Jorge Cruz at University of Brasilia, specialist course on psychoanalysis.

239 Nadia Bossa, *Psicopedagogia no Brasil: contribuições a partir da prática* (Brazil: Editora Artmed): 10.

240 Personal communication with Mário Alletti at University of Brasilia, specialist course on psychoanalysis.

241 Personal communication with Jorge Cruz at University of Brasilia, specialist course on psychoanalysis.

242 The dialogue on knowledge is a thesis presented in two of Morin's books: *Os sete saberes necessários à Educação do Futuro* (Brazil: Instituto Piaget) and *O pensar complexo* (Brazil: Editora Garamond).

243 Personal communication with Edgar Morin at Conferência em seminário de verão realizado pelo Centre Nacional de la Recherche Scientifique, Niort, France, 2008.

Contributors

J. Baird Callicott is University Distinguished Research Professor and formerly Regents Professor of Philosophy at the University of North Texas. He is the co-Editor-in-Chief of the *Encyclopedia of Environmental Ethics and Philosophy* and author or editor of a score of books and author of dozens of journal articles, encyclopedia articles, and book chapters in environmental philosophy and ethics. Professor Callicott has served the International Society for Environmental Ethics as President and Yale University as Bioethicist-in-Residence, and he has served the UNT Department of Philosophy and Religion Studies as chair. His research goes forward simultaneously on four main fronts: theoretical environmental ethics, comparative environmental ethics and philosophy, the philosophy of ecology and conservation policy, and biocomplexity in the environment, coupled natural and human systems (sponsored by the National Science Foundation). Professor Callicott is perhaps best known as the leading contemporary exponent of Aldo Leopold's land ethic and is currently exploring an Aldo Leopold Earth ethic in response to global climate change. He taught the world's first course in environmental ethics in 1971 at the University of Wisconsin-Stevens Point. His teaching at UNT includes graduate and undergraduate courses in ancient Greek philosophy and ethical theory.

Satish Kumar, a former monk and long-term peace and environment activist, has been quietly setting the global agenda for change for over 50 years. Inspired in his early twenties by the British peace activist Bertrand Russell, he embarked on an 8,000-mile peace pilgrimage. Carrying no money and depending on the hospitality of strangers, he walked from India to America, via Moscow, London and Paris, to deliver a packet of 'peace tea' to the leaders of the world's four nuclear powers. In 1973, Kumar settled in the United Kingdom, taking up the post of editor of *Resurgence* magazine, a position he has held ever since. During this time, he has been the guiding spirit behind a number of now internationally respected ecological and educational ventures including the Schumacher College in South Devon, where he is still a Visiting Fellow. In his 50th year, Kumar undertook another pilgrimage, again carrying no money. This time, he walked 2,000 miles to the holy places of Britain, in celebration of his love of life and nature. In July 2000 he was awarded an Honorary Doctorate in Education from the University of Plymouth. In July 2001, he received an Honorary Doctorate in Literature from the University of Lancaster; in November 2001, he was presented with the Jamnalal Bajaj International Award for promoting Gandhian values outside India. Kumar's autobiography, *No Destination*, has sold over 50,000 copies. He is also the author of *You Are, Therefore I Am: A Declaration of Dependence, The Buddha and the Terrorist* and *Earth Pilgrim*. Dr Kumar is on the advisory board of Our Future Planet, a unique online community sharing ideas for real change. He continues to teach and run workshops on reverential ecology, holistic education and voluntary simplicity.

Tim O'Riordan is Emeritus Professor of Environmental Sciences at the University of East Anglia. He received an OBE in 2010. He holds an MA in Geography from the University of Edinburgh, an MS in Water Resources Engineering from Cornell University, and a PhD in Geography from the University of Cambridge. He has edited a number of key books on the institutional aspects of global environmental change, policy and practice, led two international research projects on the transition to sustainability in the European Union (1995–2002) and edited two editions of the textbook *Environmental Science for Environmental Management*. Professor O'Riordan is European Advisor to the UK Sustainable Development Commission and a member of Sustainability East, the East of England Sustainable Development Round Table. His research deals with the themes associated with better governance for sustainability. He is also active in the evolution of sustainability science partnerships. His direct work relates to designing future coastlines in East Anglia in England so that they are ready for sea-level rise. and the creation of sound economies and societies for a sustainable future. He is a core member of the Prince of Wales' seminar on Business and the Environment and is an assessor for the Prince of Wales Accounting for Sustainability project. He sits on the Corporate Responsibility Body for Asda plc, and also on the Growth and Climate Change Panel for Anglian Water Group. Professor O'Riordan is Executive Editor of *Environment* magazine. His other research interests cover interdisciplinary approaches to pursuing the transition to sustainability, risk perception and communication, business and social virtue.

José Lima Santos was born in Lisbon in 1963; he has a degree in agronomy from the Technical University of Lisbon, 1987; a PhD from the University of Newcastle upon Tyne, 1997; and a habilitation degree from the Technical University of Lisbon, 2008. He is currently Professor of Environmental Economics at the Institute of Agronomy, Technical University of Lisbon. His main research and teaching areas are the economic valuation of the environment, cost–benefit analysis of public policy, policy analysis, and agri-environment policy design and evaluation. He has worked as an OECD expert on the Economic Valuation of Biodiversity (1998/9) and the Multifunctionality of Agriculture (Washington workshop, 2000). He was Director General of the Agri-Food Planning and Policy Bureau, Ministry of Agriculture, in charge of policy design and evaluation, as well as European and external affairs, between 2000 and 2003, and was main policy negotiator in the 2003 Common Agricultural Policy (CAP) reform. He has been a member of the National Council on the Environment and Sustainable Development (CNADS) since 2006 and was a member of the Consultative Committee of the Gulbenkian Environmental Program from 2007 to 2011. Professor Santos is the author of *The Economic Valuation of Landscape Change: Theory and Policies for Land Use and Conservation* (1998) and a contributor to the following volumes: *Environmental Valuation, Volume II* (1999); *Towards Policies for Rural Amenities: Valuing Public Goods and Externalities* (2000); *Environmental Value Transfer: Issues and Methods* (2007); *Conservación de la Naturaleza y Actividad Económica* (2008); and *Environment at the Crossroads* (2010).

Marina Silva (born 1958) is a Brazilian environmentalist and politician. Orphaned at age 16, young Marina moved to the state capital, Rio Branco. She graduated in history from the Federal University of Acre at 26 and became increasingly politically active. In 1994, Ms Silva was the first rubber tapper ever elected to Brazil's Federal Senate. She was a member of the Partido dos Trabalhadores (until August 2009). Marina Silva was appointed Brazil's Environment Minister by President Lula in his first term (2003). She resigned mid-May in 2008. On 19 August 2009, Silva announced her switch from the Workers' Party to the Green Party. Marina Silva has received numerous awards including, in 1996, the Goldman Environmental Prize for South and Central America. In 2007, the United Nations Environment Program named her one of the Champions of the Earth, and the same year the *Guardian* newspaper considered her to be one of the 50 people who could save the planet. She was the winner of the 2009 Sophie Prize. Running in the 2010 Brazilian elections, Marina Silva won 19.4% of the popular vote.

Viriato Soromenho-Marques (born 1957) teaches in the Departments of Philosophy and European Studies of the University of Lisbon, where he is Full Professor. He is member of the Lisbon Academy of Sciences. He was Vice-Chair of the European Environmental and Sustainable Development Advisory Council's network (2001–06), being a member of the Portuguese Council (CNADS). He was the scientific coordinator of the Gulbenkian Environment Program (2007–11). He was a member of the Advisory Group on Energy and Climate Change by invitation of the President of the European Commission (2007–10).

Sofia Guedes Vaz graduated as an environmental engineer in 1989. She worked in environmental consultancy and received an MSc in environmental technology in 1993 from Imperial College, London. From 1997 to 2002 she worked at the European Environment Agency in Copenhagen, specialising in environmental policy and environmental emerging issues such as the precautionary principle. From 2003 to 2007 she undertook a PhD on environmental political philosophy, focusing on responsibility and virtue politics. Sofia co-edited the books *Late Lessons from Early Warnings: The Precautionary Principle 1896–2000* (2001) and *Interfaces between Science and Society* (2006) and co-authored the *Environmental Ethics Handbook* (2010). She is currently a researcher on sustainable consumption and on food waste at CENSE (the Centre for Environmental and Sustainability Research), New University of Lisbon. She is part of the group 'Stand-Up Scientists', who communicate science through stand-up comedy. Sofia writes a monthly column entitled 'Positive Environment' for a Portuguese online magazine. She has two children and lives in Portugal.

Index

For Product Safety Concerns and Information please contact our EU
representative GPSR@taylorandfrancis.com
Taylor & Francis Verlag GmbH, Kaufingerstraße 24, 80331 München, Germany

www.ingramcontent.com/pod-product-compliance
Ingram Content Group UK Ltd.
Pitfield, Milton Keynes, MK11 3LW, UK
UKHW021028180425
457613UK00021B/1108